THE CBT Handbook
Cognitive Behavioural Therapy

Catherine Evans-Jones

Published by **Speechmark Publishing Ltd**, 70 Alston Drive, Bradwell Abbey, Milton Keynes MK13 9HG, UK

Tel: +44 (0)1908 326 944   Fax: +44 (0)1908 326 960

www.speechmark.net

Copyright © Catherine Evans-Jones, 2011

All rights reserved. The whole of this work, including all text and illustrations, is protected by copyright. No part of it may be copied, altered, adapted or otherwise exploited in any way without express prior permission, unless it is in accordance with the provisions of the Copyright Designs and Patents Act 1988 or in order to photocopy or make duplicating masters of those pages so indicated, without alteration and including copyright notices, for the express purposes of instruction and examination. No parts of this work may otherwise be loaded, stored, manipulated, reproduced, or transmitted in any form or by any means, electronic or mechanical, including photocopying and recording, or by any information, storage and retrieval system without prior written permission from the publisher, on behalf of the copyright owner.

002-5660/Printed in the United Kingdom by CMP

British Library Cataloguing in Publication Data
A catalogue record for this book is available from the British Library

ISBN 978 0 86388761 1

Contents

Introduction

Purpose of the book	2
Introduction to cognitive behavioural therapy	2
Using the worksheets	3
Contents of the book	4

Chapter 1 Preparing for and ending therapy

Worksheet summaries	6
Assessment	8
Preparing to make changes	10
My list of problems and goals	11
Reviewing progress	12
Preparing for the next session	13
Learning from setbacks	14
Becoming my own therapist	15
Summarising what I've learned	16
Reducing the likelihood of relapse	17

Chapter 2 Cognitive behavioural therapy techniques

Worksheet summaries	20
Understanding what's keeping the problem going	27
Understanding the development of difficulties and strengths	28
Drawing out the development and maintenance of difficulties	30
Drawing out the development and maintenance of strengths	31
Understanding possible triggers	32
Solving problems	33
Noticing and recording my thoughts (1)	34
Noticing and recording my thoughts (2)	35
Evaluating my thoughts – helpful questions	36
Evaluating my thoughts – my responses	37
Evaluating my thoughts – my favourite questions	38
Thought distortions	39
Noticing my thought distortions	40
Evaluating my thought distortions – helpful questions	41
Evaluating my thought distortions – my responses	42
Building up the evidence for an alternative thought or belief	43
Evaluating my thought – using a 0%–100% scale (1)	44

Evaluating my thought – using a 0%–100% scale (2)	45
Working out who was responsible	46
Preparing to work with images and memories	47
Working with images and memories	48
Testing out my thoughts – conducting behavioural experiments	49
A diary of behavioural experiments	50
Carrying out a survey	51
Identifying my unhelpful coping strategies	53
How helpful are my coping strategies? Keeping a diary	54
How helpful are my coping strategies? Advantages and disadvantages	55
Testing out a new coping strategy	56
Drawing up a ladder of behaviours	57
Working my way up the ladder of behaviours	58
Noticing where my attention is	59
Distracting myself	60
Working out my assumptions and beliefs (1)	61
Working out my assumptions and beliefs (2)	62
Evaluating the advantages and disadvantages of my assumptions and beliefs	63
Imagining the effects of a helpful assumption or belief	64
Changing my unhelpful assumptions and core beliefs	65
Daily record of my belief	66
Finding helpful memories	67
Evaluating the past differently	68
Evaluating my belief – a role play	69

Chapter 3 Depression

Worksheet summaries	72
Drawing out my experiences of depression	74
My experiences of depression	75
Recording rumination for one day	76
Recording rumination for one week	77
Disrupting rumination	78
Keeping a diary of my activities	79
Evaluating my activity diary	81
Finding activities that give me pleasure and a sense of achievement	82
Predicting pleasure and a sense of achievement	83
Doing things step-by-step	84
Evaluating thoughts which make me less active	85

Chapter 4 Anxiety

Worksheet summaries	88
4.1 Overview	
Drawing out my experiences of anxiety	97
My experiences of anxiety	98
Analysing my fear	99
Evaluating my fear	100
Evaluating the probability of my fears	101
Imagining the worst	102
Exposing myself to situations I fear	103
Identifying my safety behaviours	104
Listing my safety behaviours	105
Experimenting with my safety behaviours	106
Practising relaxation	107
4.2 Panic	
My experiences of panic	108
Recording my experiences of panic	109
Identifying my fears which lead me to panic	110
Testing out my physical sensations of anxiety	111
4.3 Worry or generalised anxiety disorder	
My experiences of worry	112
Recording worry for one day	113
Recording worry for one week	114
Understanding why I worry	115
Deciding what to do about my worries	116
Planning time to worry	117
How realistic are my worries?	118
Learning to tolerate uncertainty	119
4.4 Obsessive-compulsive disorder (OCD)	
My experiences of obsessive-compulsive disorder	120
Recording my obsessions and compulsions	121
Recording a compulsion for one day	122
Recording a compulsion for one week	123
Identifying my fears about thoughts	124
Evaluating explanations for my difficulties – OCD	125
Exposing myself to my intrusive thoughts	126
Testing out whether thoughts can cause things to happen	127

Recording changes in my compulsions	128
Recording situations when I don't neutralise	129

4.5 Health anxiety

My experiences of health anxiety	130
Finding alternative explanations for physical sensations	131
Evaluating the likely seriousness of physical sensations	132
Evaluating explanations for my difficulties – health anxiety	133

4.6 Social anxiety

My experiences of social anxiety	134
Recording social situations	135
Evaluating my thoughts in social situations	136
Experimenting with focusing on myself	137
Using video or audio feedback	138

4.7 Post-traumatic stress disorder (PTSD)

My experiences after trauma	139
Identifying things that make me remember the trauma	140
Listing triggers to memories of the trauma	141
Grading traumatic memories	142
Managing memories of the trauma	143
Evaluating guilt – helpful questions	144
Evaluating guilt – my responses	145

Chapter 5 Other presenting problems

Worksheet summaries	148

5.1 Low self-esteem

Drawing out my experiences of low self-esteem	150
My experiences of low self-esteem	151
Recording self-criticism for one day	152
Recording self-criticism for one week	153
Answering self-critical thoughts	154
Evaluating my self-worth	155
Identifying good things about me	156
Building up evidence of my good points	157

5.2 Sleep

Keeping a sleep diary	158
Analysing my sleep diary	159

References 161

Index 163

Introduction

Introduction

Purpose of the book

This book aims to provide cognitive behavioural therapists with a comprehensive set of worksheets which they can photocopy and use with adult clients. A range of worksheets have been brought together so that therapists can easily access a variety of tools. As well as attempting to cover the 'basic' techniques of cognitive behavioural therapy (CBT), it also has worksheets specific to presenting problems, for example, obsessive-compulsive disorder (OCD), panic and worry. It is assumed that practitioners will already have an understanding of cognitive behavioural principles and be looking for practical aids for therapy. Therapists will need a clear understanding of cognitive behavioural principles, core therapy skills, a good therapeutic relationship and a good cognitive behavioural formulation before such worksheets can be used helpfully, and therefore ethically, with clients. Therapists will then be able to pick and choose which worksheets could be helpful for their clients.

Introduction to cognitive behavioural therapy

The aim of CBT is to help people overcome their emotional difficulties through helping them identify and change their thoughts and behaviour. The word 'cognitive' refers to thoughts, images, memories and attention. The emotional difficulties for which people might seek CBT are varied, for example, depression, phobias or worry. The behaviours which can be consequences and causes of such emotional difficulties can also vary; they include reduced activity levels, avoidance of social situations or excessive cleaning.

CBT was developed from the theories of Ellis (eg Ellis, 1957, 1961, 2001) and Beck (eg Beck, 1963, 1964; Beck et al, 1979). They proposed that it is people's interpretations of situations that cause distress and therefore also their associated coping behaviour. For example, someone who views themselves as a failure (cognition) may feel ashamed and depressed (emotions) and avoid others (behaviour). Such coping behaviour may then reinforce the interpretations and distress. For example, avoiding others gives the person less opportunity to receive positive feedback from others. Thus the person becomes stuck in a vicious cycle. The cognitive behavioural model proposes that people can identify such vicious cycles in their current lives and then change their thoughts and behaviours in order to reduce their distress; for example, selecting occasions when they feel able to meet people (behaviour) and consequently receive positive feedback which then changes their view of themselves (cognition). Helping clients to identify the historical causes of such interpretations and coping strategies can give them the message that their beliefs and behaviours can be viewed as understandable outcomes given their past experiences, while also acknowledging that such beliefs and behaviours may not be the most useful ones now. Thus therapy can be an opportunity where the client begins to develop interpretations and behaviours which are more helpful in their current circumstances in that they cause them less distress and/or impairment.

CBT has been evaluated for a wide range of presenting problems, and evidence of its efficacy has been found for depression, panic, agoraphobia, generalised anxiety disorder

(GAD), specific phobias, social phobia, obsessive-compulsive disorder (OCD) and post-traumatic stress disorder (PTSD) (Roth and Fonagy, 2004). The National Institute for Health and Clinical Excellence (NICE) has recommended CBT as one of the psychological treatments of choice for depression (NICE, 2004b), panic, agoraphobia, GAD (NICE, 2004a), PTSD (NICE, 2005b) and OCD (NICE, 2005a).

Expansion of CBT continues. Many new adaptations are being devised and researched; for example, expanding its use to clients with diagnoses of personality disorder, incorporating the practice of mindfulness and developing techniques to work at a meta-cognitive level. This book will not include these newer theories, but instead will focus on the 'basic' techniques developed and validated for common psychological problems such as anxiety and depression.

Using the worksheets

Worksheets are essential tools in CBT. They can have many purposes, for example, recording events and patterns, providing new information and suggesting new ways of thinking and acting. It is not expected that therapists will use all of the worksheets with each client; rather they will pick and choose which worksheets could be helpful. When and how to use a worksheet is determined by a number of factors, such as the formulation, the stage in therapy, the current focus of treatment, the reading and writing ability of the client and the wishes of the client.

Before you use a worksheet, some useful questions to consider may be:

- What are the current focus and goals of therapy?
- How might this worksheet help with the focus and goals?
- Is it possible to predict some of the difficulties which this client might experience when using this worksheet?
- What can be done to overcome these difficulties?
- Are there any reasons not to use this worksheet with my client?
- What does my client need to know in order to understand the purpose of this worksheet?

After giving out worksheets, check that the client understands their purpose and how they will use them, for example, by asking, 'Can you explain to me how you think this worksheet might be useful for you?' Elicit any concerns, for example, by asking, 'Can you predict any difficulties in using this worksheet? What can we do about that?" In the subsequent therapy session find out about their experiences of using the worksheet. Did it fit the intended purpose? If not, do you know why not? Does it need to be adapted or should an alternative worksheet be used? If it was useful, then what has the client learned? What will they do next as a result? Do they want to use the worksheet again?

The use of worksheets in CBT is an ongoing learning process for both therapists and clients.

Some worksheets may be given as homework while others may be started or completed in sessions with the therapist. Therapists need to consider whether clients fully understand the worksheets and are capable of completing them on their own, or whether they may need assistance in sessions to understand and complete them.

Contents of the book

The first chapter of this book contains worksheets for use in helping clients prepare for starting and ending therapy. Chapter 2 focuses on generic 'basic' CBT techniques which are used throughout the course of therapy. The next three chapters focus on different presenting problems and the techniques associated with them: depression (Chapter 3), anxiety (Chapter 4) and other presenting problems (Chapter 5).

👥 This symbol indicates when the therapist is addressing the client.

Chapter 1
Preparing for and ending therapy

Worksheet summaries

The following worksheets are to be used at assessment:

Assessment

This worksheet is not to be given to clients but instead to be used by therapists to help them to consider what information they may want to collect at assessment. After completing an assessment, information can be put into the relevant categories in order to aid therapists' analysis and understanding.

Preparing to make changes

This worksheet may help clients to consider their reasons for why they want to change as well as to problem-solve potential obstacles to making changes. Hopefully, this can aid motivation and be useful information to reflect back on as therapy progresses and should clients struggle with motivation.

My list of problems and goals

This worksheet is divided up into 'Thoughts', 'Feelings', 'Behaviours', 'Physical' and 'Other' in order that clients can have clear and useful goals that are relevant to the cognitive behavioural model they will be working within. Rating scales for each aspect may be useful.

The following worksheets are to be used during therapy:

Reviewing progress

During therapy clients can regularly refer back to their *My list of problems and goals* worksheet in order to identify any progress. This can be recorded on the *Reviewing progress* worksheet and then used to consider what the next goal is for therapy.

Preparing for the next session

Just before a session, for example, the evening or morning before, clients can complete this worksheet. It may help clients to summarise important points and consequently aid both therapists and clients in identifying what to work on that session.

Learning from setbacks

Should clients have a setback in therapy, that is, a significant increase in their distress, then they can use this worksheet in order to be able to reflect on and learn from their experiences. It can be a helpful tool in giving clients the message that setbacks are likely and can be useful learning opportunities.

Becoming my own therapist

When there is a longer time frame between sessions, for example, two to four weeks, then clients might find it useful to set aside regular time to do their own 'self-therapy' sessions. This involves reflecting on what they've been trying to achieve, how they've done, how they understand issues from a CBT perspective and devising an action plan for the remaining time before the next session. This may help clients to develop the skills necessary for becoming their own therapist.

The following worksheets are to be used towards the end of therapy:

Summarising what I've learned

Towards the end of therapy, clients can summarise what they've learned in order to be able to reflect back on this information once the sessions have ended. They could plan where to store the worksheet so that it is accessible and easily remembered; for example, stuck up somewhere, in the top drawer of a desk or in their bag.

Reducing the likelihood of relapse

In this worksheet clients identify their thoughts, feelings and behaviours at different levels of relapse so that they might be more likely to recognise them should they experience them in the future. Different strategies may be appropriate at different levels of relapse and so identifying these in advance might make clients more likely to remember and use them. As well as considering where to put the worksheet so that it is accessible, they can identify people who could own copies of the worksheet, for example, family, friends and health professionals. These people might be able to identify relapse, engage in helpful strategies and encourage the client to engage in helpful strategies.

The CBT Handbook: Cognitive behavioural therapy

Assessment

Therapists: Use the following headings to help organise the information you have gathered during assessment.

Presenting problems: What are the problems? Triggers? Modulating factors?
Mood/emotions: What emotions are problematic for the client? How severe are they?
Cognitions: What thoughts/memories/images do they have? Where's their attention?
Physical responses: What physical responses do they have?
Behaviour – unhelpful: What coping strategies are unhelpful, that is, keep the problem going?
Behaviour – helpful: What coping strategies are helpful, that is, lead to helpful thinking?
Current medication: What medication are they taking and at what dosage?

(P) This page may be photocopied for instructional use only © Catherine Evans-Jones

Functioning/impact of problems: How do the problems affect their relationships, work, finances and/or physical health?

Substance misuse: Do they abuse substances such as alcohol and/or drugs?

Risk assessment: What are the risks to themselves, others and children?

Background to the problem: When did the problem start and how has it changed over time?

General background/childhood: What is relevant from their childhood and life until now?

Previous interventions: Have they had previous experience of medication, therapy, etc?

Goals: What are their goals for therapy? Short–medium–long-term?

Motivation to change: What are their reasons for change? What might reduce their motivation?

Ability to use CBT: How able are they to use CBT ideas, for example, in terms of understanding, focus and time?

Other: Is there any other relevant information?

Preparing to make changes

Identify what the possible advantages and disadvantages are of staying as you are now and of making helpful changes.

	Advantages	Disadvantages
Remaining the same		
Making helpful changes		

Which to me are the most important advantages of helpful change?
What might I be able to do in order to overcome the possible disadvantages of making helpful changes?
Are there any images, metaphors, song lyrics or quotes that will help inspire me?
How can I help myself to remember this when I need to motivate myself?

My list of problems and goals

The more specific you are in identifying problems and goals, the easier it is to focus on what to change and on what you want to achieve. Goals are most useful when they are SMART:

Specific   **M**easurable   **A**chievable   **R**ealistic   **T**imebound

Consider the following question: If you woke up one morning and you no longer had your current difficulties, if they had suddenly disappeared, how would things be different? What would you be thinking, feeling and doing? Use the following categories to identify some problems and goals.

	Problems	Goals
Thoughts		
Feelings		
Behaviours		
Physical		
Other		

Which goals are most important to you? Put numbers next to them to indicate this, that is, 1 = most important, 2 = second most important, etc.

Reviewing progress

Look over your goals and identify what progress you have made against them. How have things improved? What is your next focus for each goal?

Date: _____

	Progress made to date	Next step
Thoughts		
Feelings		
Behaviours		
Physical		
Other		

Which goals are most important for you? Put numbers next to them to indicate this, that is, 1 = most important, 2 = second most important, etc.

Preparing for the next session

Thinking through the following questions can help you to be prepared for your next session and will hopefully make it a more useful experience for you.

What did I learn and find helpful from my most recent therapy session?

Was there anything that was less helpful/unhelpful about my most recent session?

What were the tasks we agreed I would do this week?

What tasks have I been able to do since my last therapy session?

What happened when I did them and what have I learned? Were there obstacles?

How have I been feeling since the last session?

What therefore seems important to discuss at my next therapy session?

Learning from setbacks

👥 When you think you are having a setback, answer the following questions in order to find helpful strategies for the present and for the future.

How am I feeling? _____

What physical sensations am I having? _____

What am I thinking? _____

What am I doing? _____

What seemed to be the trigger(s) to this setback? _____

How did the trigger(s) affect me? _____

Can I draw a sketch of the vicious cycle I seem to be in?

What is making it difficult to get out of the vicious cycle I am in? _____

What have I tried before when I've been feeling like this?	
Helpful strategies	
Unhelpful strategies	

What else could I do? What CBT techniques could I use? _____

What have I learned from this setback? _____

How can I use what I've learned? What will I do? _____

Becoming my own therapist

👥 Towards the end of therapy your sessions may be more spread out, giving you more time to try out new ideas. In-between therapy sessions you could review what has been happening for you using the questions below.

Today's date: _____ Date of my most recent therapy session: _____

What did I learn and find helpful from my most recent therapy session?
What were the tasks we agreed I would do before the next session?
How have I been feeling since my most recent therapy session?
Which tasks have I been able to do?
What have I learned from them?
Have there been any particularly difficult situations since my most recent therapy session?
How can I understand them using a CBT model?
What could I do to overcome these difficulties? What CBT techniques could I use?
Overall, what progress have I made against my goals for therapy?

When is my next therapy session?	
What could I try out before then?	
What would I be hoping to learn/achieve from doing that?	

Are there any obstacles I can predict? What can I do about them?

Summarising what I've learned

What do I now understand about why and how my problems developed?

What do I now understand about what kept my problems going?

What CBT strategies have I learned? In what way have they been useful?	
CBT strategy	**How it has been useful**

How has my thinking changed?

How has my behaviour changed?

What do I need to do in order to keep making progress?

What are my goals?	
Short-term, for example, next few months	
Medium-term, for example, 3–12 months	
Long-term, for example, 12 months and onwards	

Reducing the likelihood of relapse

What are the situations which might lead to a setback for me?

What could I do to help me cope with these situations?

At different levels of relapse how would I be and what would be helpful coping strategies?

Level of relapse	Thoughts (T), feelings (F), behaviour (B)	Coping strategies I could use	What others could do
Mild	T: F: B:		
Moderate	T: F: B:		
Severe	T: F: B:		

Would looking at my *Summarising what I have learned* worksheet help right now? How?

Who do I need to tell about these ideas?

Where do I need to put this plan so that I can see it regularly and/or find it easily?

How often will I look at this plan? How will I remember to do that?

Chapter 2
Cognitive behavioural therapy techniques

Worksheet summaries

There are a number of worksheets that draw out formulations, for example *Understanding what's keeping the problem going, Drawing out my experiences of depression, Drawing out my experiences of low self-esteem*. Completed formulation worksheets can be kept in sight during sessions, for example, on a table between the therapist and client. Therefore, they can be referred back to and revised as relevant information is discovered. As well as identifying difficulties it can be helpful for clients to identify their strengths and resilience which have helped them to cope with their difficulties.

Understanding what's keeping the problem going

This diagrammatic formulation is one way in which clients can identify the factors currently maintaining their difficulties. This may allow them to see the vicious cycle which they are in.

Understanding the development of difficulties and strengths

This worksheet can be used to help clients understand how their difficulties and strengths have developed over time and so help them make sense of their current experiences. A good formulation gives the message 'it makes sense how you are now because of what happened to you'.

Drawing out the development and maintenance of difficulties

Drawing out the development and maintenance of strengths

The information identified in the previous two worksheets can be combined in these two worksheets.

Understanding possible triggers

This worksheet suggests possible events which might have occurred around the time that clients' difficulties began or worsened. Clients are encouraged to consider how any identified events affected them and this information can be added into the formulation.

Solving problems

For many problems, clients can benefit from going through a structured format whereby they identify the problem and any possible solutions before choosing and reviewing the effectiveness of the best solution.

Noticing and recording my thoughts (1)

This worksheet guides clients through a fundamental task of CBT: identifying distressing thoughts. Ideally, clients record this information during or just after they are distressed.

Noticing and recording my thoughts (2)

Once clients have used the *Noticing and recording my thoughts (1)* worksheet sufficiently to learn how to identify their distressing thoughts they can go on to use this worksheet which allows more space for information to be recorded.

The following worksheets can be used together: *Evaluating my thoughts – helpful questions, Evaluating my thoughts – my responses, Evaluating my thoughts – my favourite questions, Thought distortions, Noticing my thought distortions, Evaluating my thought distortions – helpful questions, Evaluating my thought distortions – my responses.*

Evaluating my thoughts – helpful questions

Once clients have identified distressing thoughts, they can read through the list of questions on this worksheet; this may help clients to evaluate the thoughts.

Evaluating my thoughts – my responses

Clients can record their answers to the questions in *Evaluating my thoughts – helpful questions* on this worksheet. They use one copy of the worksheet to evaluate one thought.

Evaluating my thoughts – my favourite questions

In order to make the process of evaluating thoughts more efficient clients can build up a list of their favourite questions on this worksheet.

Thought distortions

Clients are referred to this worksheet when using the *Evaluating my thoughts – helpful questions* worksheet. It lists and explains some common thought distortions.

Noticing my thought distortions

Once clients have understood the various thought distortions listed in the *Thought distortions* worksheet, they can keep a diary of their own. Every time they notice a distressing thought they can identify which thought distortion(s) they might be making.

Evaluating my thought distortions – helpful questions

Once clients have understood the different thought distortions and learned to identify their own, they can progress on to reading through this list of questions which may help them to evaluate their thought distortions.

Evaluating my thought distortions – my responses

Clients can record their answers to the questions in the worksheet *Evaluating my thought distortions – helpful questions* on this worksheet. They use one copy of the worksheet to evaluate one thought.

Building up the evidence for an alternative thought or belief

In order to strengthen alternative/helpful thoughts or beliefs, supporting evidence can be noticed and recorded over time in this worksheet.

The following worksheets involve various verbal, that is, not behavioural, strategies for evaluating thoughts and beliefs: *Evaluating my thought – using a 0%–100% scale (1)*, *Evaluating my thought – using a 0%–100% scale (2)*, and *Working out who was responsible*.

Evaluating my thought – using a 0%–100% scale (1)

Percentage scales can be used to evaluate particular qualities that may be referred to in core beliefs or rules for living; for example, 'I am worthless' (worth), 'others are dangerous' (safety), and 'I must be perfect' (perfectionism). Clients develop their own scale and anchor points for the quality and then rate aspects of themselves/others/their life on this scale. Therapists can help clients to identify good aspects of the quality which they may demonstrate but not easily recognise in themselves.

Evaluating my thought – using a 0%–100% scale (2)

This worksheet again evaluates a particular quality that may be referred to in core beliefs or rules for living. Clients consider what factors make up this quality and rate themselves on this scale. Therapists can help clients to notice any cognitive biases affecting this process.

Working out who was responsible

This can be a useful worksheet when clients appear to be attributing to themselves a lot of responsibility for past or current events/circumstances. Clients can be aided in reattributing this responsibility. Clients develop a reasonable list of other people and factors who could also be responsible and then divide up the responsibility between them. This may help them to attribute less responsibility to themselves.

The following worksheets may be useful when working with images: *Preparing to work with images and memories,* and *Working with images and memories.*

Preparing to work with images and memories

Before doing any direct imagery work, therapists can use this worksheet with clients to identify what the original image consists of and how it could be changed in helpful ways.

Working with images and memories

Each time imagery work is carried out clients can complete this worksheet to record their experiences and learning.

Testing out my thoughts – conducting behavioural experiments

Whenever a client conducts a behavioural experiment they can record their experiences and what they've learned on this worksheet. The first half of the worksheet sets out why and how the behavioural experiment will be carried out while the second half explores what happened and what was learned.

A diary of behavioural experiments

When multiple behavioural experiments are being carried out, in order to evaluate one main thought or belief, clients can use this worksheet. They can keep track of their level of conviction in their original and alternative thoughts.

Carrying out a survey

Using this worksheet can help clients to make best use of a survey by asking them to consider what they want to know from the survey, how they'll get that information, and, afterwards, what they've learned from it.

The following worksheets can be used to work with clients' coping strategies: *Identifying my unhelpful coping strategies*, *How helpful are my coping strategies? Keeping a diary*, *How helpful are my coping strategies? Advantages and disadvantages*, and *Testing out a new coping strategy*.

Identifying my unhelpful coping strategies

An initial step is likely to be helping clients to identify their coping strategies. This worksheet uses a list of common unhelpful coping strategies to help them to begin this process.

How helpful are my coping strategies? Keeping a diary

Clients can use this worksheet to notice what strategies they used, how it affected their mood and any other consequences.

How helpful are my coping strategies? Advantages and disadvantages

Clients can identify the possible short-term and long-term advantages and disadvantages of each coping strategy.

Testing out a new coping strategy

When clients test out new coping strategies they can record the outcome in this worksheet – it may help clients to evaluate the usefulness of such coping strategies.

Drawing up a ladder of behaviours

Clients who want to enter into a particular distressing or difficult situation may find it helpful to break down this process into increasingly more difficult stages. The concept of a 'ladder' is used to illustrate this approach and to help clients to identify different levels on the ladder.

Working my way up the ladder of behaviours

As clients do the things listed on the *Drawing up a ladder of behaviours* worksheet they can record their experiences and learning on this worksheet.

Noticing where my attention is

Clients can learn to recognise how much of their attention is on different aspects of a situation. They do this by allocating a percentage amount of attention to themselves, the task and their environment. Combined, these three percentage amounts should add up to 100%, for example, 50% on self, 30% on environment and 20% on task. Clients are encouraged to notice any links between their attention and their mood.

Distracting myself

This worksheet can be used by clients to draw up a list of activities which distract them and can then be kept for reference for when they want to try to distract themselves.

The following worksheets can be used to identify and work with assumptions and core beliefs: *Working out my assumptions and beliefs (1)*, *Working out my assumptions and beliefs (2)*, *Evaluating the advantages and disadvantages of my assumptions and beliefs*, *Imagining the effects of a helpful assumption or belief*, *Changing my unhelpful assumptions and core beliefs*, *Daily record of my belief*, *Finding helpful memories*, *Evaluating the past differently*, and *Evaluating my belief – a role play*.

Working out my assumptions and beliefs (1) and (2)

These worksheets use a variety of questions in order to help clients to identify possible assumptions and core beliefs they may hold. The second worksheet focuses on identifying the underlying meaning behind a situation in order to identify any related assumptions and beliefs.

Evaluating the advantages and disadvantages of my assumptions and beliefs

Once clients have identified possible alternative assumptions and beliefs they can consider the advantages and disadvantages of their original and their alternative beliefs.

Imagining the effects of a helpful assumption or belief

Clients can consider in detail what it might be like to live their life if they held their alternative beliefs with a higher degree of conviction. This may increase their motivation to make changes.

Changing my unhelpful assumptions and core beliefs

This worksheet asks clients to evaluate their original assumptions and beliefs before moving on to consider the effects of alternative beliefs and how they might build up evidence for, and remember, them.

Daily record of my belief

In order to notice any changes in how much clients believe their assumptions or core beliefs (helpful or unhelpful) they can rate their maximum and minimum percentage conviction each day and notice any links to particular situations.

Finding helpful memories

Clients are asked to recall memories which support alternative assumptions or core beliefs in order to build up evidence for them.

Evaluating the past differently

Clients can identify memories which may have been viewed as evidence for unhelpful assumptions and beliefs in a different, possibly more adult, way in order that such memories may no longer support the unhelpful assumptions and beliefs.

Evaluating my belief – a role play

In order to evaluate their assumptions and beliefs clients and therapists may carry out a role play in which one person defends an unhelpful belief and the other person challenges it. Before doing this, clients can identify some of the arguments which both sides may make (as well as spontaneously identifying more during the role play itself). The last three questions on the worksheet help the person to reflect on what they've learned after completing the role play.

Understanding what's keeping the problem going

In order to be able to make helpful changes you need to understand what is keeping the problem going. Try to identify the following things and write them in the boxes below.

Situation. In what situation do I often experience the difficulty?

Where am I? What am I doing? Who else is there?

When is it?

Thoughts. What am I thinking when I am in that situation?

What's the worst thing about the situation?

Feelings. How am I feeling? What one word sums this up?

Physical sensations. What physical sensations do I have?

Behaviour. What do I do? How do I cope?

Consequences. What happens as a result of what I do?

Environment. What is the context that affects the problem?

Environment

Situation

Thoughts

Consequences

Feelings/Physical sensations

Behaviour

Understanding the development of difficulties and strengths

It is useful to see how key experiences have led you to develop certain beliefs about yourself, others and the world, and how these beliefs then affect what you expect from situations and how you approach them. Try to identify the following things.

Early experiences	What experiences (good and difficult) shaped how I think about myself, others and the world? What memories stand out as important and/or powerful? Think about when I started to believe my core beliefs or assumptions.
Core beliefs	What do I think about myself, for example, when upset? How would I finish the following sentence: 'I am ....'? What do I think about others? How would I finish the sentence: 'Others are ....'? What do I think about the world? How do I expect it to be? How would I finish the sentence: 'The world is ....'?
Assumptions/Rules	From these core beliefs what do I expect from others and myself? For example, how would you finish the sentences: 'I must ....', 'Others should ....', 'If I do .... then .... will happen.'?
Coping strategies/ behaviours	From my core beliefs and rules for living, what strategies have I learned that help me cope? What do I do when I'm distressed? What do I do to try to prevent myself becoming distressed?

Now put these ideas into the boxes on the following page. Think about those experiences, beliefs, rules and strategies which might be keeping your difficulties going: put these into the boxes on the left-hand side. Also think about those experiences, beliefs, rules and strategies which have helped you to cope and be resilient – what have been your strengths? Put these into the boxes on the right-hand side.

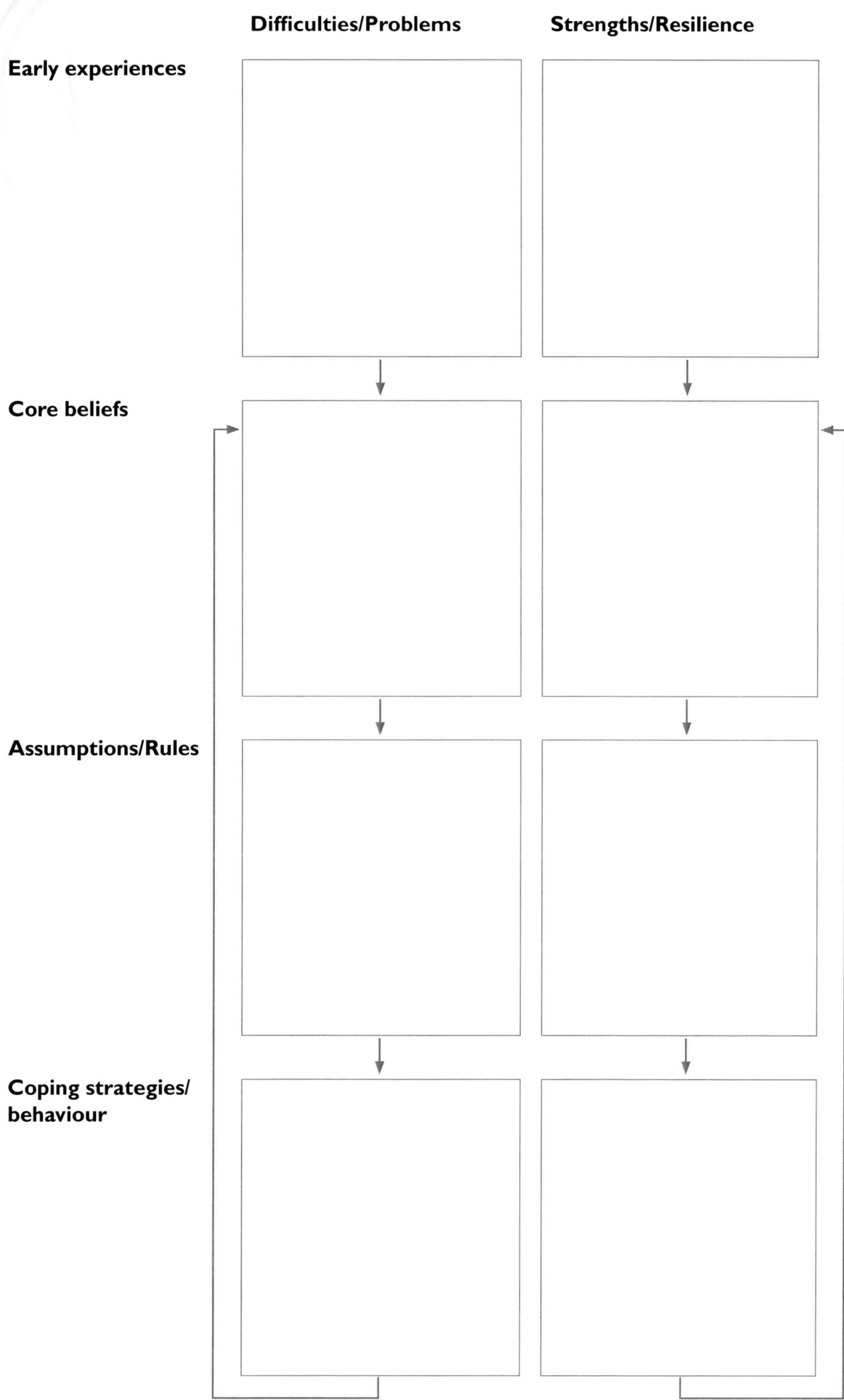

Drawing out the development and maintenance of difficulties

Below is a model of how emotional difficulties can develop and then keep going. Consider how your experiences might fit into this model and write your ideas in the boxes.

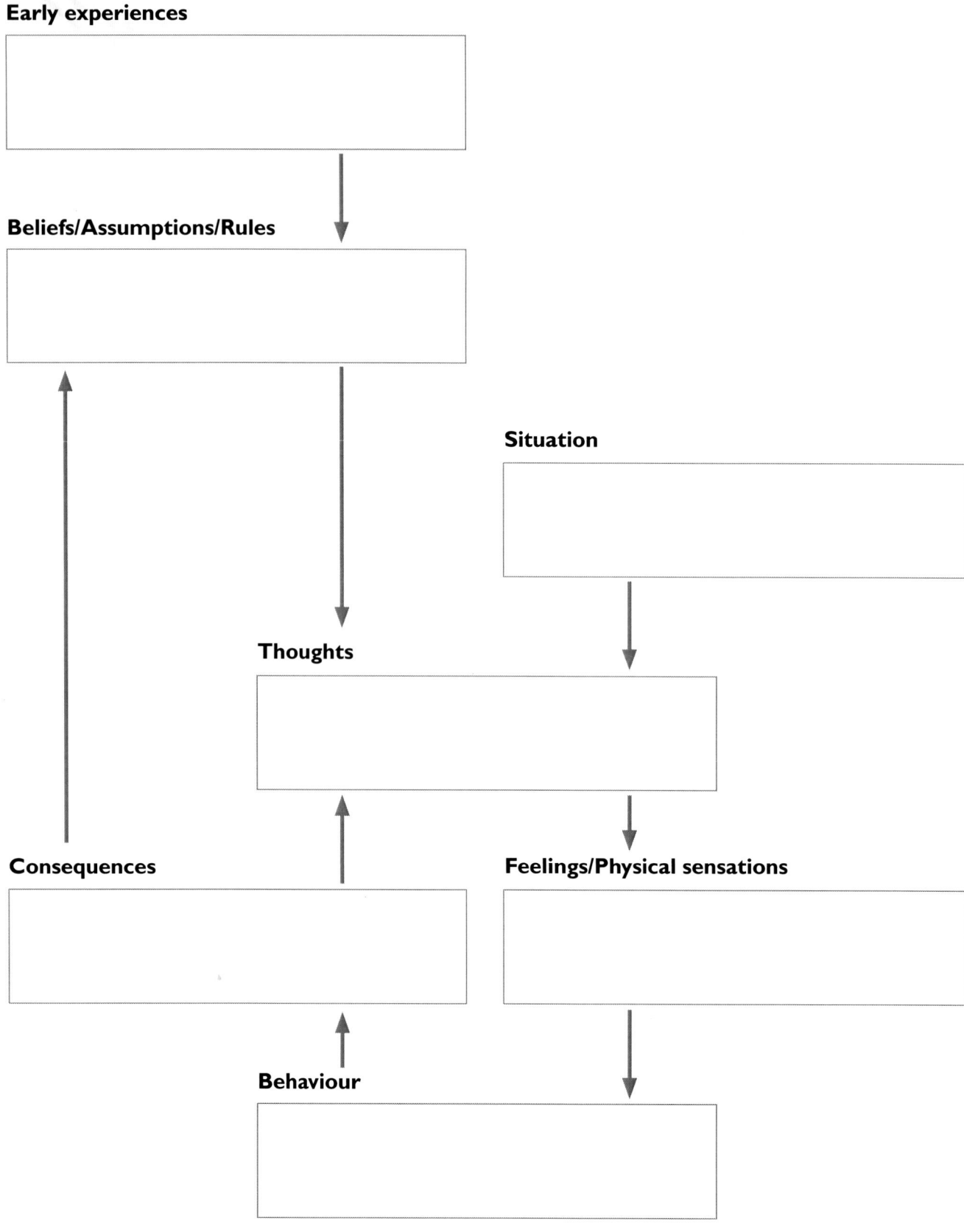

Drawing out the development and maintenance of strengths

Below is a model of how emotional resilience and strength can develop and then keep going. These are the things which have helped you to cope with your difficulties. Consider how your experiences might fit into this model and write your ideas in the boxes.

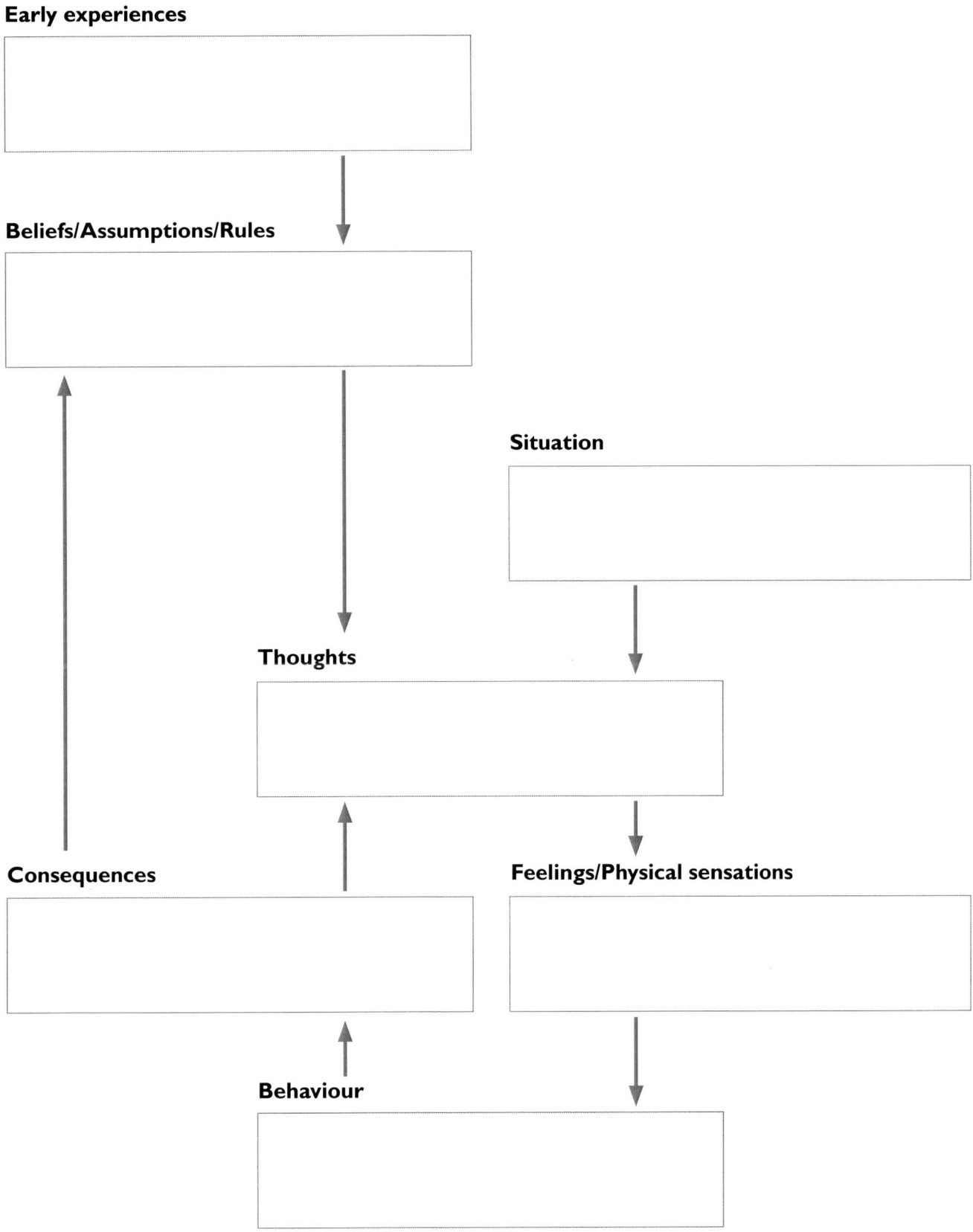

Understanding possible triggers

Use the following checklist to identify any things which happened around the time that your distress started and/or got worse.

Event/Possible trigger	Did this happen to me?	If so, when?
Moving house	Yes/No	
Starting a new job	Yes/No	
Important changes at work	Yes/No	
Redundancy/Retirement	Yes/No	
Financial problems	Yes/No	
Illness/Accident	Yes/No	
Death of/injury to a loved one	Yes/No	
Relationship problems	Yes/No	
Sexual difficulties	Yes/No	
Being a victim of crime	Yes/No	
Taking tests/exams	Yes/No	
Other	Yes/No	
Other	Yes/No	
Which were the most upsetting situations?		
How did they affect me?		

Solving problems

When you need to find ways of solving a problem go through the following steps either on your own or with someone else.

Today's date: _____

What is the problem?	

What possible solutions are there? Include as many as you can think of. Work out the advantages and disadvantages of each possible solution.

Possible solution	Advantages	Disadvantages

Weighing up the advantages and disadvantages of each solution, number them according to how helpful they are, for example, 1 = best option, 2 = second best option, 3 = third best option, etc.

What seems like my best option at the moment?	
What is this option in detail? What will happen? Where? When? With whom?	
What possible problems might there be with this course of action?	
What would I do if such problems happened?	
Date when I will review this plan of action:	
Review: What happened?	
How helpful was that?	
Do I need to choose another option? If so, which one?	

Noticing and recording my thoughts (1)

Whenever you notice yourself experiencing a negative mood, for example, feeling sad, anxious, angry, low or ashamed, write down the following information.

Situation. What was happening and when and where? Who was I with?

Mood. What emotion was I feeling? Usually these are one word, such as 'sad', 'angry' or 'anxious'. How strongly did I feel the emotion out of 10?

Thoughts. What was I thinking at the time? Imagine a thought bubble: What would it have in it? Write thoughts in sentences, for example: 'I won't enjoy it', 'He shouldn't have done that', 'I can't cope.' How strongly do I believe each thought out of 100?

Situation	Mood (0–10)	Thoughts (0%–100%)

What situations tend to make me feel distressed?

Which emotion(s) do I tend to have which upset me?

What thoughts do I tend to have? Which are helpful and which are unhelpful?

Noticing and recording my thoughts (2)

Use this worksheet to record more of your unhelpful thoughts.

Situation	Mood (0–10)	Thoughts (0%–100%)

Evaluating my thoughts – helpful questions

Use the first four questions to clarify which thought you are evaluating and how you are feeling. Write your answers on the worksheet *Evaluating my thoughts – my responses*.

1. What is my unhelpful thought?
2. How much do I believe it between 0% and 100%?
3. What emotions do I feel because of having this thought?
4. How strongly do I feel each of them from 0 to 10?

Now use these questions to help you evaluate your unhelpful thought.

1. What do I mean exactly?
2. What is the 'evidence' *for* my thought? What would a lawyer say who was arguing *in favour of* my unhelpful thought? What suggests my thought might be true?
3. What is the 'evidence' *against* my thought? What would a lawyer say who was arguing *against* my unhelpful thought? Is any of the 'evidence' in favour of my thought not good quality evidence? In what way? What suggests my thought might *not* be true?
4. Given the facts, is there another way to view the situation?
5. What distortions am I making? How could I question these? Can I use the *Thought distortions* worksheets?
6. What would I say to myself if I felt OK?
7. Have I thought differently about this at another time?
8. How might I think about this situation in five years' time?
9. What is a more helpful way to view the situation?
10. What do I think is the worst that could happen? How could I cope with this?
11. How have I coped in this situation before? What helped?
12. What strengths do I have that might help me in this situation?
13. What could others do to help?
14. What could I do to make the situation better?
15. What would some of my friends and/or family say to me if they knew what I was thinking?
16. What would I say to a friend or family member if they told me that they were thinking this?

- What conclusions have I reached?
- How much do I now believe my unhelpful thought between 0% and 100%?
- How strongly do I now feel the accompanying emotions from 0 to 10?

Put an asterix (*) next to those questions which you found most helpful and go on to the *Evaluating my thoughts – my favourite questions* worksheet.

Evaluating my thoughts – my responses

👥 Read through the questions in the worksheet *Evaluating my thoughts – helpful questions*. Choose one unhelpful thought and write down your responses to the questions.

My unhelpful thought:		
How much I believe my thought:		0%–100%
My emotion(s) and how strongly I feel them:		0–10

My responses to the questions:

1	
2	
3	
4	
5	
6	
7	
8	
9	
10	
11	
12	
13	
14	
15	
16	

What conclusions have I reached?		
How much do now I believe the unhelpful thought?		0%–100%
How strongly do I now feel the emotions listed above?		0–10

Evaluating my thoughts – my favourite questions

Once you have practised evaluating a few of your thoughts using the *Evaluating my thoughts* and the *Evaluating my thought distortions* worksheets, write down the questions which you find most helpful.

Question 1:	
Question 2:	
Question 3:	
Question 4:	
Question 5:	
Question 6:	
Question 7:	
Question 8:	

How can I remember these questions when I'm distressed?

Thought distortions

When people are distressed they might be making some of the following common thought distortions.

Catastrophising.	Predicting that the worst will happen, that a catastrophe will occur.
Fortune-telling.	Predicting that the future will turn out a particular way.
All-or-nothing thinking.	Seeing things as either one way or another. There is no middle ground: things are either good or bad.
Over-generalising.	Reaching general conclusions based on little evidence/few examples.
Ignoring the positives.	Not paying attention to or ignoring the positive facts in situations, for example, ignoring compliments, not recognising successes or strengths.
Focusing on the negatives.	Paying attention to the negative facts in a situation.
Scanning.	Looking out for what you are fearful of.
Mind-reading.	Assuming that you know what people are thinking with insufficient evidence to support your conclusions.
Labelling.	Giving yourself (or others) negative and global labels that are typically one word, for example, 'stupid', 'incapable'.
Shoulds.	Having rigid and/or unrealistic rules for yourself and/or others which are often expressed as 'I should …' 'They should …' 'I shouldn't …' 'They shouldn't …'
Self-blame.	Blaming yourself for something which isn't your fault or which is only partly your fault.
Emotional reasoning.	Using your feelings rather than facts to judge a situation.

Noticing my thought distortions

Using the *Thought distortions* worksheet to help you, keep a diary of what unhelpful thoughts you have and what thought distortions you think you might be making.

Situation	Mood	Thoughts	Thought distortions

Which thought distortions do I tend to make?
How do they make me feel?

Evaluating my thought distortions – helpful questions

Use the following questions to evaluate the thoughts distortions which you have made. Write your responses on the worksheet *Evaluating my thought distortions – my responses*.

Catastrophising.	What other possible (less awful) outcomes could there be? How have things turned out before in similar situations? Is there anything to suggest that the worst-case scenario is unlikely to happen? If it did happen, how would I cope and how would I think and feel about it in one year's time? Would there be anything positive to gain from it having happened?
Fortune-telling.	Are there facts to suggest that this might happen? Is it possible to know what will happen? Are other outcomes possible and more likely?
All-or-nothing thinking.	What's a more balanced, middle-of-the road view? On a scale of 0% to 100% where would I rate the thought?
Over-generalising.	What's a more realistic conclusion based on the evidence in this situation? Are there exceptions to the general conclusion I have come to?
Ignoring the positives.	What are some of the positives in the situation? What are some of my strengths? What positives might someone else see in the situation or in me? What would it mean to be able to notice the positives?
Focusing on the negatives.	What other aspects of the situation am I not focusing on? What other aspects of the situation might someone else focus on?
Scanning.	What else is there in the situation which I might not be noticing? What could be helpful to focus on?
Mind-reading.	Is there any evidence to suggest what people might be thinking? What else might they be thinking? Is this how they tend to think about me? How could I cope if they were thinking this about me?
Labelling.	Is it helpful to call myself or others this? Is it true? What is a more balanced view of myself or others? Specifically what has happened? What have I done? Are there some aspects of me or others which don't seem to fit this label?
Shoulds.	Is this an unrealistic and/or unhelpful expectation? Would I expect this of others? Would others expect this of me? Is it possible to achieve this goal all the time?
Self-blame.	Could there be other causes of the situation? Could my share of the responsibility be less than I first thought? Would other people see me as being to blame as what I do?
Emotional reasoning.	Can I reach different conclusions about the situation depending on whether I go by my feelings or by facts? What do the facts suggest? What might I be thinking if I felt better?

Evaluating my thought distortions – my responses

👥 Read through the questions in the worksheet *Evaluating my thought distortions – helpful questions*. Choose one unhelpful thought, identify which thought distortions you are making and write down your responses to the questions for those thought distortions.

My unhelpful thought:		
How much I believe my thought:		0%–100%
My emotion(s) and how strongly I feel them:		0–10

Thought distortion	My responses to the questions for that thought distortion

What conclusions have I reached?		
How much do now I believe the unhelpful thought?		0%–100%
How strongly do I now feel the emotions listed above?		0–10

Building up the evidence for an alternative thought or belief

Once you have evaluated a thought or belief you can make a regular note of any evidence to support the alternative thought or belief. You may do this over some weeks and months.

My alternative thought:	

Date	Evidence to support my alternative thought or belief	How strongly I believe the alternative thought or belief (0%–100%)

What conclusions can I make from all this evidence?

What have I learned? How can I use what I've learned? What will I do?

Evaluating my thought – using a 0%–100% scale (1)

👥 For some thoughts it can be helpful to think of them on a scale of 0% to 100%, for example, when you are rating a desired quality in yourself or others, such as 'kindness' or 'success', or when you are rating an all-or-nothing thought, such as, 'My life's worthless.'

What is the quality/thought which I am rating?	
Where would I put myself/the thought on a scale of 0% to 100%?	

Work out some behaviours or other factors which represent this quality/thought at 0%, 25%, 30%, 75% or 100%. For example, if you were rating kindness you might put 'giving regular donations to charity' under the 75% column and 'only ever thinking of oneself' under the 0% column.

0%	25%	50%	75%	100%

What examples are there from your own life of this quality/thought? Give each one a rating from 0% to 100% according to the scale you have devised above.	%

Now re-rate where you would put yourself/the thought on the 0% to 100% scale:	

What have I learned from this exercise?	

What have I learned? How can I use what I've learned? What will I do?

Evaluating my thought – using a 0%–100% scale (2)

Here is another way to use a 0%–100% scale to evaluate a thought.

| What is the quality/thought which I am rating? | |

Where would I put myself/the thought on a scale of 0% to 100%? Put a mark on the line below to represent this.

0% _____ 100%

Now think of what makes up the quality or thought you are rating. For instance, what makes someone a kind person (for example, giving to charity, helping friends), what makes someone's life worthwhile (for example, success at work, good relationships)? For each of these aspects rate where you would put yourself/your thought on a scale of 0% to 100% by putting a mark on the line. List as many aspects as you can.

The aspect I am rating:

0% _____ 100%

0% _____ 100%

0% _____ 100%

0% _____ 100%

0% _____ 100%

0% _____ 100%

0% _____ 100%

Now re-rate where you would put yourself/the thought on the 0% to 100% scale by taking an average of all the marks you have made. Put a mark on the line below to represent this.

0% _____ 100%

What have I learned from this exercise?
What have I learned? How can I use what I've learned? What will I do?

Working out who was responsible

This exercise is to help you consider who or what was responsible for a particular event or situation.

What is the situation or event I am evaluating responsibility for?	

List all of the people and factors which contributed to that situation happening. Make the list as long as possible; include even seemingly small contributing factors. If you think that you were in some way responsible for the situation then put yourself at the bottom of the list.

Next, go through the list giving each factor a percentage out of 100 to represent how much it contributed to the situation. In total, all the percentage scores must add up to 100. Alternatively, draw slices of pie in the pie chart below to represent how responsible each factor was – the bigger the slice of pie the bigger the amount of responsibility.

Factors in some way responsible	Percentage of responsibility (0–100%)
	%
	%
	%
	%
	%
	%

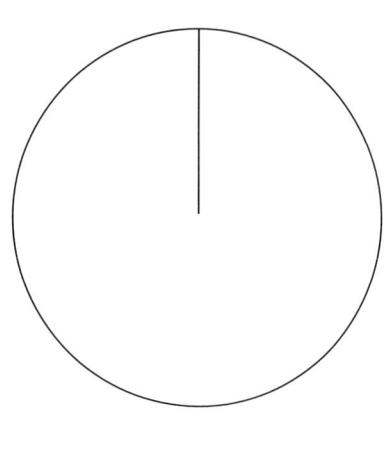

Were the answers what I expected?	
If not, what do I make of that? Why do I think that is?	

What factor(s) seemed most responsible?	
What level of responsibility did I give myself?	
What does this mean to me?	
Do I think that other people would give different ratings? What might they be?	

What have I learned from this exercise?	
How can that be useful for me?	
Will I think or do anything differently as a result of this exercise?	
What have I learned? How can I use what I've learned? What will I do?	

Preparing to work with images and memories

You may work together with your therapist to change images and/or memories in sessions. In order to prepare for this you can answer the following questions.

What is the image or memory? Describe it in as much detail as possible:	
What?	
Where?	
When?	
Who?	
What was I thinking?	
What was I feeling?	
What was I doing?	
What else is in the image or memory?	
What unhelpful thought(s)/beliefs(s) does this image or memory lend support to?	
How does it do this?	
When I was in the situation what did I need to have happen, to make me feel: safe/better/happy?	
What could I have done or said?	
What could others have done or said?	
What could have happened instead?	
Is it possible to fast-forward the image until I get to a point where I feel OK?	
How could the image or memory be made humorous?	
What would the image look like on a TV screen in the distance? What would I see?	

Caution: Traumatic memories can be very distressing when thought about in detail. You may need to do this work in session with your therapist.

Working with images and memories

Use this worksheet to notice what happens before, during and after work done on changing images and/or memories.

What image or memory is being changed?

What is the accompanying unhelpful thought or belief? How much do I believe it from 0%–100%?

How did I change the image?

How did I feel as I was doing this?

How much do I now believe the accompanying unhelpful thought or belief?

Is there an alternative, more helpful thought or belief? How much do I believe this thought from 0%–100%?

What have I learned? How can I use what I've learned? What will I do?

Caution: Traumatic memories can be very distressing when thought about in detail – you may need to do this work in session with your therapist.

Testing out my thoughts – conducting behavioural experiments

👥 When carrying out behavioural experiments it's good to prepare well for them beforehand and to reflect on what you have learned afterwards. Use the following questions to help you do this.

What is the automatic thought I am testing out?	

How much do I believe this?	%	
What alternative thoughts might there be and how much do I believe them		%
How will I test out my thought(s)?		
• What will I do?		
• Where?		
• When?		
• With whom?		
• What will I look out for?		
What problems might there be and how will I cope with them?		

👥 Carry out the experiment and then answer the following questions.

What happened?	
How does this relate to the thought(s) I was testing out?	
How much do I now believe my automatic thought(s)?	
What alternative thoughts might there be and how much do I believe it 0–100%?	
What do I need to do next to carry on testing out my thought(s)?	

A diary of behavioural experiments

👥 Over time you might do a number of behavioural experiments which are all testing out a particular thought. Keep a diary of what happened each time and note down how much you believe your original and alternative thoughts.

What is the unhelpful thought I am testing out?

What are the alternative thoughts?

Date	Experiment	What happened	How much I believe my original thought(s) (0%–100%)	How much I believe my alternative thought(s) (0%–100%)

What have I learned? How can I use what I've learned? What will I do?

Carrying out a survey

Sometimes you might want to find out about other people's opinions and experiences on a particular subject. In preparation for doing this, answer the following questions.

What belief/assumption/thought am I trying to explore?

How much do I believe this at the moment?	%

What do I want to find out from people?

What questions will help me to do this?

What information do I need to find out about them, for example, age, gender?

Who am I going to give the survey to, for example, friends, therapist's colleagues?

Is it going to be anonymous, that is, the respondents don't know who I am and/or I don't know who they are?

Has someone else checked to see that the questions make sense?

What potential pitfalls do I need to be aware of when doing this, for example, focusing more on particular answers than others, or interpreting answers in an unhelpful way?

What are my predictions about what people will say?

👥 Carry out the survey and then answer the following questions.

How can I summarise what people said?

Was there anything which surprised me?

What have I learned?

How does this relate to my original belief/assumption/thought?

How much do I now believe my original belief/assumption/thought?

What have I learned? How will I use what I've learned? What will I do?

Identifying my unhelpful coping strategies

Below are some common potentially unhelpful coping strategies. Note down which of these you have used in the past and which ones you continue to use now.

Unhelpful coping strategy	Have I used it in the past?	Do I use it now?
Comfort eating		
Drinking alcohol		
Using non-prescription drugs		
Inappropriately taking prescription drugs		
Avoiding phone calls		
Staying in bed a lot		
Staying at home a lot		
Seeing friends or family less		
Smoking more		
Exercising less		
Avoiding public or busy places		
Leaving situations when feeling uncomfortable		
Not going into new situations		
Going out only with someone else		
Relying on others a lot more		
Getting others to do things for me a lot more		
Asking others for reassurance a lot		
Other		

What have I learned? How can I use what I've learned? What will I do?

How helpful are my coping strategies? Keeping a diary

Making a note of how you cope when you are feeling distressed can be a good way to work out which strategies might be helpful and which might not. Whenever you notice yourself experiencing a negative mood, for example, feeling sad, anxious, angry, low or ashamed, write down the following information.

Situation. What was happening, when and where? Who was I with?

Mood during. What emotions was I feeling? Usually these are one word, for example, 'sad', 'angry' or 'anxious'. Rate how strongly you felt the emotion out of 10.

Coping. What did I do in the situation? How did I try to improve things?

Consequences. What happened as a result of what I did to try to cope?

Mood after. How did I feel after I had done something to cope? Re-rate your moods out of 10.

Situation	Mood (0–10)	Coping/What I did	Consequences	Mood after (0–10)

How do I tend to react / cope?	
Which coping strategies tend to be unhelpful?	
Which coping strategies tend to be helpful?	
What have I learned? How can I use what I've learned? What will I do?	

How helpful are my coping strategies? Advantages and disadvantages

Once you have identified some of your typical coping strategies, use the following questions to evaluate how helpful they are. Think about how it affects the following:

- your mood
- your confidence
- the situation
- your home life
- your energy levels
- other people
- your work life
- your finances.

My coping strategy:	

	Advantages	Disadvantages
Short-term		
Long-term		

Overall, what is the usefulness of my coping strategy?	
What have I learned? How can I use what I've learned? What will I do?	

Testing out a new coping strategy

As you develop new coping strategies note down what happens when you use them.

New coping strategy 1:	
Situation in which I used my new coping strategy.	What happened?

New coping strategy 2:	
Situation in which I used my new coping strategy.	What happened?

New coping strategy 3:	
Situation in which I used my new coping strategy.	What happened?

What have I learned? How can I use what I've learned? What will I do?

Drawing up a ladder of behaviours

In therapy you might be trying to go into certain situations that you find difficult. To do so, you can break down the situation into a series of steps. You can then start by planning how to take the first step. Work out what the different steps of the situation might be and then give each one a rating from 0 to 10 for how difficult or distressing it would be, where 10 is the most difficult or distressing and 0 is not difficult or distressing at all.

What situation do I want to be able to go into? What do I want to be able to do?

Level of distress/ difficulty		Step on the ladder
Hardest	10	
	9	
	8	
	7	
	6	
	5	
	4	
	3	
	2	
	1	
Easiest	0	

Working my way up the ladder of behaviours

👥 Make a note of every time you go into one of the situations on your ladder. Record what you did and rate how strongly you felt your emotion out of 10. Think about what happened and what you learned.

Date	Step (0–10)	What I did	Emotion (0–10)	What happened	What I learned

Have I come across any difficulties doing the various steps on the ladder?

What have I done about this?

What have I learned from all of the above experiences?

How can I use what I've learned? What will I do?

Noticing where my attention is

It can be helpful to become more aware of where your attention is. Are you focusing on what is happening around you (environment), on what you are doing (task) or on what you are thinking and feeling? Does this affect how you feel? Use the following diary to help you identify what you pay attention to.

Date	Situation	Attention on myself (0%–100%)	Attention on task (0%–100%)	Attention on environmnent (0%–100%)	Emotions (0–10)

What patterns are there in my attention?

Are there any links between where my attention is and how I feel?

What do I want to try to do differently in the future?

What have I learned? How can I use what I've learned? What will I do?

Distracting myself

👥 Your therapist will work with you to think about how and when distraction may be useful to you. It can be helpful to have a 'menu' of distractions from which you can choose when you need to. Activities which are most distracting tend to be the ones in which you feel absorbed. Work out how distracting you find each activity on a scale of 0 to 10 where 10 is the most distracting possible and 0 is not distracting at all.

Activities	Level of distraction (0–10)
Reading, for example, newspaper, magazine, book	
Crosswords and puzzles	
Counting, for example, number of red tops people are wearing	
Focusing on what's happening around you, for example, conversations	
Remembering something in a lot of detail	
Being creative, for example, painting, drawing	
Writing, for example, a letter, email, diary	
Cooking, for example, with a recipe to follow	
Sports, for example, football, tennis, badminton, squash, table tennis	
Others	

👥 **Caution:** Sometimes we think that an activity is distracting when it isn't, for example, watching TV or doing the ironing. During these types of activities it can be easy for your mind to wander, and therefore they are not good at distracting you. Which activities don't absorb/distract you?

Working out my assumptions and beliefs (1)

Answer the following questions to help you work out what some of your assumptions and beliefs might be.

What themes have you and your therapist noticed in your work to date?

Finish the following statements:
• I am
• Others are
• The world is
What rules and expectations do you have for:
• Yourself?
• Others?
Finish the following statements:
• I should
• I shouldn't
• Others should
• Others shouldn't
• The world should
• The world shouldn't

Did your family or other people close to you have any sayings as you were growing up? For example, 'Always do your best', 'Always be on time', etc.

Working out my assumptions and beliefs (2)

From a situation in which you were distressed it can be possible to work out underlying core beliefs and assumptions which you hold and which might be influencing how you think in that situation. Answer the following questions to see if they help you work out your underlying beliefs.

Situation:	
Emotions:	
Thoughts:	

If my expectation/fear/prediction did happen, what would be the most upsetting aspect of that?

If my thought were true, what is the worst bit about it?

If that were then true, what would that mean about me/others/the future?

What does that tell me about my expectations for myself/others/the world?

Having answered these questions, what seems to be some of my underlying beliefs and/or assumptions in this situation?

Evaluating the advantages and disadvantages of my assumptions and beliefs

Once you have identified an unhelpful core belief or assumption and an alternative core belief or assumption, consider what the advantages and disadvantages are of both.

Unhelpful core belief or assumption

Advantages	Disadvantages

Alternative core belief or assumption

Advantages	Disadvantages

What seems to be the most helpful core belief or assumption?

How can I overcome the disadvantages of the helpful core belief or assumption?

What have I learned? How can I use what I've learned? What will I do?

Imagining the effects of a helpful assumption or belief

👥 In order to assist you with acting according to your helpful assumption or belief, answer the following questions.

What is the alternative and helpful core belief or assumption?
How would I be different if I believed this more?
What would I be thinking?
What would I be feeling?
What would I be doing?
How would I be different in the following situations?
• With family?
• With friends?
• In relationships?
• At work?
• Doing my hobbies/interests
What have I learned? How can I use what I've learned? What will I do?

Changing my unhelpful assumptions and core beliefs

For each of your unhelpful assumptions and core beliefs it can be helpful to have a summary of all that you have learned about them.

What is my assumption/belief?
What experiences made me believe my assumption/belief?
In what situations does my assumption/belief influence me?
How do I feel when I believe my assumption/belief?
How do I act when I believe my assumption/belief? What do I do?
What is unhelpful about all of these things?
What experiences suggest that my assumption/belief may not always be true?
What is a more helpful assumption/belief?
How do I feel when I believe my helpful assumption/belief?
What do I do when I believe my helpful assumption/belief?
What are the consequences of how I act when I believe my more helpful assumption/belief?
What can I do to find more evidence for my helpful assumption/belief?
How can I try to remember my helpful assumption/belief?

Daily record of my belief

👥 Once you have identified a belief (helpful or unhelpful) which you hold, then make a note of the following things.

My belief:	

Day of the week		What was happening	How much I believed it (0%–100%)
Monday	When did I believe it most today? When did I believe it least today?		
Tuesday	When did I believe it most today? When did I believe it least today		
Wednesday	When did I believe it most today? When did I believe it least today		
Thursday	When did I believe it most today? When did I believe it least today		
Friday	When did I believe it most today? When did I believe it least today		
Saturday	When did I believe it most today? When did I believe it least today		
Sunday	When did I believe it most today? When did I believe it least today		

What tends to be happening when I believe my belief the most?

What tends to be happening when I believe my belief the least?

Finding helpful memories

Unhelpful core beliefs and assumptions can mean that helpful memories get ignored or forgotten. Bringing out these memories and placing them at the forefront of your mind may help you make changes in your unhelpful beliefs.

Pick a helpful core belief or assumption and look for memories of events which support it.

What is my alternative, helpful core belief or assumption?	
How much do I believe it on a scale of 0%–100%?	

Experience	How it supports my alternative belief

How much do I now believe my alternative belief on a scale of 0%–100%?	
What have I learned? How can I use what I've learned? What will I do?	

Evaluating the past differently

👥 Things happened to you as a child which now, as an adult, you might have a different way of understanding. Pick one of your assumptions, rules or core beliefs and re-evaluate a few key childhood experiences. Think about how you would reinterpret them now in a way which might not confirm your beliefs.

What is my core belief, assumption or rule?

Childhood experience	How I made sense of it then – what it told me about me/others/the world	How I understand it now as an adult

What have I learned? How can I use what I've learned? What will I do?

Evaluating my belief – a role play

👥 You and your therapist can understand and challenge a belief using role play. One of you role plays being the belief and the other person role plays challenging the belief. To prepare for this, think of some of the things which both of you might say.

What the belief might say in order to defend itself:
•
•
•
•
•
•
What the other person might say or ask in order to challenge the belief:
•
•
•
•
•
Having carried out the role play, what conclusions can I reach?
What have I learned through doing the role play?
How can I use what I've learned? What will I do?

Chapter 3
Depression

Worksheet summaries

Drawing out my experiences of depression

This worksheet can be used by clients to help them understand what is maintaining their depression using a cognitive behavioural formulation.

My experiences of depression

Clients can use this checklist to help them consider whether their experiences are typical of depression as well as to identify whether such experiences have happened in the past and/or now.

Recording rumination for one day / one week

It can be helpful for clients to notice how often and in what situations they are ruminating, that is, repetitively thinking about distressing issues in a non-productive manner. They can choose whether to keep a diary of their ruminating for one day or for one week. The purpose of the diaries is not to capture the content of the rumination but rather to notice each time it happens. They can then begin to explore patterns in their rumination and links with their mood.

Disrupting rumination

After considering how they might disrupt rumination, clients can keep of a diary of this process and how it affects their mood, allowing them to reflect on whether or how they might want to continue to disrupt their rumination.

The following worksheets can be used to help clients to identify patterns in their daily activities and then to make helpful changes in order to lift their mood: *Keeping a diary of what I do, Evaluating my activity diary, Finding activities that give me pleasure and a sense of achievement, Predicting pleasure and a sense of achievement, Doing things step-by-step, Evaluating thoughts which make me less active.*

Keeping a diary of my activities

Without changing what they are typically doing, clients can keep a diary for a week of their activities and associated levels of pleasure and achievement.

Evaluating my activity diary

Clients can use the questions in this worksheet to learn from what they wrote down and noticed in the *Keeping a diary of what I do* worksheet.

Finding activities that give me pleasure and a sense of achievement

In order to further identify which activities clients might benefit from starting or reinstating, they can answer the questions on this worksheet. They can then have a list of activities to refer back to when they are planning what to do. This can be used like a menu to pick from, for example, each day or week.

Predicting pleasure and a sense of achievement

Clients may not accurately predict how much pleasure and achievement activities will give them and this worksheet can help them to notice this. The first three columns are completed before an activity and the final three columns are completed after an activity.

Doing things step-by-step

Before engaging in a planned activity, clients can break it down into smaller, more manageable, steps, consider what resources or assistance they might need and decide when they will carry it out.

Evaluating thoughts which make me less active

When clients or therapists notice automatic thoughts which make clients less likely to be active, for example, 'There's no point', 'I won't enjoy it', these thoughts can be listed along with possible alternative, more helpful, thoughts. Clients can refer back to this worksheet when the automatic thoughts next occur in order that they may be more able to challenge them and so engage in the planned activity.

Drawing out my experiences of depression

Below is a model of depression. Consider how your experiences fit into this model.

Situation. In what situation do I tend to feel depressed? Where am I? What am I doing? Who else is there? When is it?

Thoughts. What am I thinking when I am in that situation, for example, 'I'm useless', 'Things won't improve', 'It's too much effort'?

Emotions. How am I feeling? What one word sums this up, for example, 'sadness', 'guilt', 'worthlessness', 'hopelessness', 'depression'.

Physical sensations. What physical sensations do I have, for example, lethargy?

Behaviour. What do I do? How do I cope, for example, avoidance, doing less, putting off tasks and/or thinking a lot about my problems?

Consequences. What happens as a result of what I do, for example, less enjoyment, feeling worse and/or problems building up?

Environment. What is the context that affects the problem?

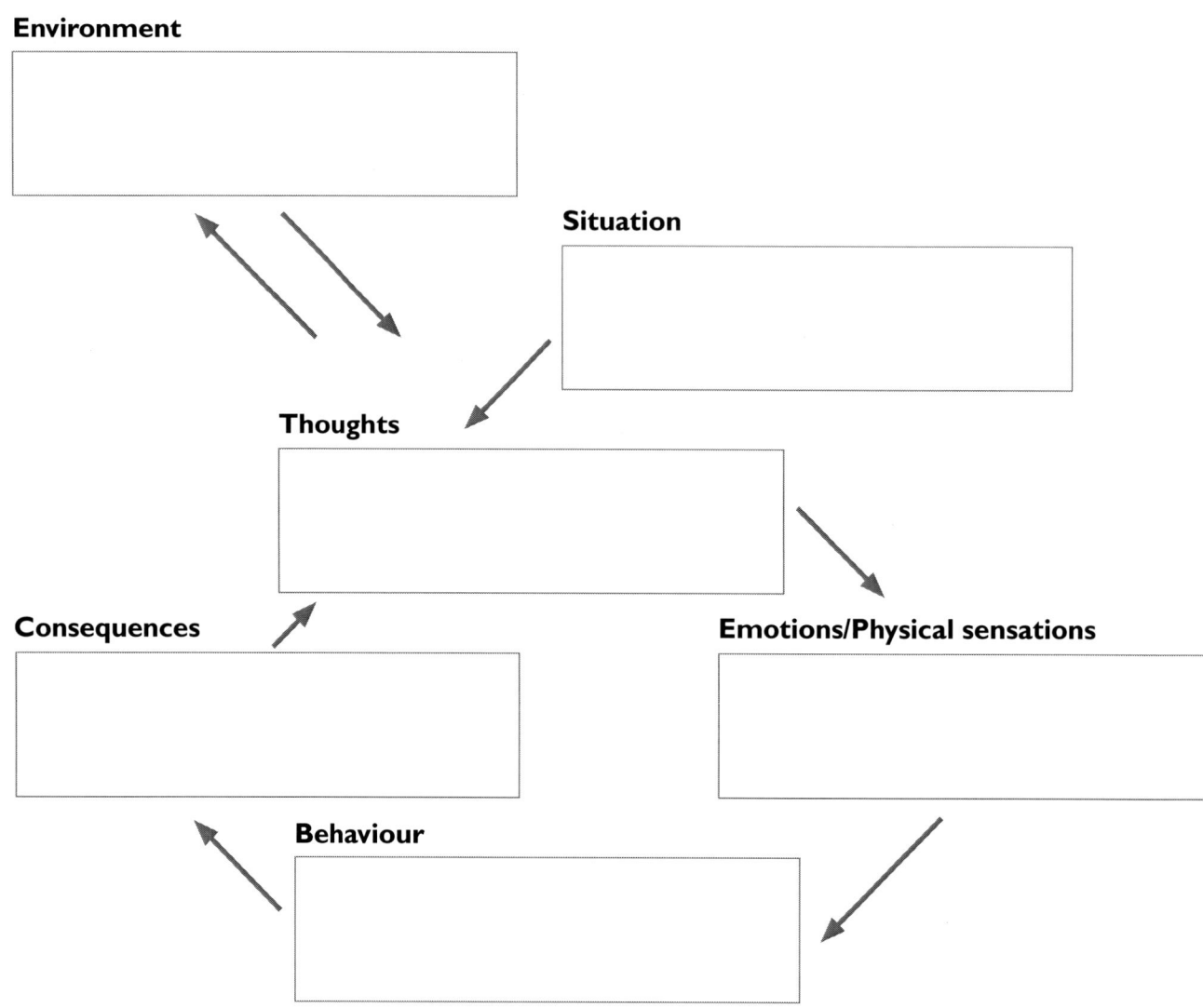

My experiences of depression

Below is a list of common experiences for people suffering from depression. Identify which experiences of depression you have experienced recently and in the past.

Possible experiences of depression	Have I experienced this?	When?	Do I experience this now?	Comments
Feeling sad or unhappy	Yes/No		Yes/No	
Feeling worthless or guilty	Yes/No		Yes/No	
Feeling under confident	Yes/No		Yes/No	
Feeling hopeless	Yes/No		Yes/No	
Feeling helpless	Yes/No		Yes/No	
Feeling agitated or irritable	Yes/No		Yes/No	
Difficulty concentrating	Yes/No		Yes/No	
Difficulty making decisions	Yes/No		Yes/No	
Not enjoying myself	Yes/No		Yes/No	
Not looking forward to things	Yes/No		Yes/No	
Not being interested in things	Yes/No		Yes/No	
Criticising myself a lot	Yes/No		Yes/No	
Being preoccupied with how I'm feeling and my difficulties	Yes/No		Yes/No	
Thinking pessimistically	Yes/No		Yes/No	
Thinking about harming myself	Yes/No		Yes/No	
Thinking about killing myself	Yes/No		Yes/No	
Doing less than normal	Yes/No		Yes/No	
Putting off tasks or problems	Yes/No		Yes/No	
Not wanting to see or talk to people	Yes/No		Yes/No	
Doing things feels an effort	Yes/No		Yes/No	
Feeling unmotivated	Yes/No		Yes/No	
Feeling very tired	Yes/No		Yes/No	
Lying in bed a lot (more)	Yes/No		Yes/No	
Difficulties sleeping	Yes/No		Yes/No	
Crying a lot	Yes/No		Yes/No	
Changes in appetite	Yes/No		Yes/No	
Lack of interest in sex	Yes/No		Yes/No	
Neglecting my self-care	Yes/No		Yes/No	

Recording rumination for one day

Rumination involves getting caught up in negative thoughts in a manner which is unproductive and unhelpful. In order to help you to begin to step back from your rumination it can be helpful to notice how often it is happening. Keep a tally chart, where, for example, IIII = 4, of how many times you get caught up in negative thoughts and rumination over one day, dividing the day up into chunks of one hour.

Date:

Morning	Afternoon	Evening	Night-time
0600–0700	1200–1300	1800–1900	0000–0100
0700–0800	1300–1400	1900–2000	0100–0200
0800–0900	1400–1500	2000–2100	0200–0300
0900–1000	1500–1600	2100–2200	0300–0400
1000–1100	1600–1700	2200–2300	0400–0500
1100–1200	1700–1800	2300–2400	0500–0600

When did I ruminate the *most*?	
Do I know why? What was happening at the time?	
How did I feel at these times?	
When did I ruminate the *least*?	
Do I know why? What was happening at the time?	
How did I feel at these times?	
Is there anything else that I've learned?	

What have I learned? How can I use what I've learned? What will I do?

Recording rumination for one week

Rumination involves getting caught up in negative thoughts in a manner which is unproductive and unhelpful. To help you to begin to step back from your rumination it can be useful to notice how often it is happening. Keep a tally chart, where, for example, IIII = 4, of how many times you get caught up in rumination over one week.

Week starting:

	Morning	Afternoon	Evening	Night-time
Monday				
Tuesday				
Wednesday				
Thursday				
Friday				
Saturday				
Sunday				

When did I ruminate the *most*?	
Do I know why? What was happening at the time?	
How did I feel at these times?	
When did I ruminate the *least*?	
Do I know why? What was happening at the time?	
How did I feel at these times?	
Is there anything else that I've learned?	

What have I learned? How can I use what I've learned? What will I do?

Disrupting rumination

Rumination involves getting caught up in negative thoughts in a manner which is unproductive and unhelpful. Keep a diary of whenever you manage to notice that you are ruminating and then do something to disrupt it.

Date	Situation	Mood (0–10)	How I disrupted the rumination	Mood after (0–10)

What did I do that was most successful at disrupting the rumination?
What did I do that was least successful at disrupting the rumination?
How did I generally feel after disrupting the rumination?
What have I learned? How can I use what I've learned? What will I do?

Keeping a diary of my activities

Make a note of what you do every hour for one week, for example, cooking, sleeping, watching TV. For each activity rate how much *pleasure (3)* and *achievement (5)* you feel at the time on a scale of 0 to 10 where 0 = no pleasure or achievement, and where 10 = the most pleasure or achievement you can imagine feeling. For example, 'cooking dinner' may give you P = 3 and A = 5, which means feeling a small amount of pleasure when cooking dinner and a moderate sense of achievement.

	Monday	Tuesday	Wednesday	Thursday	Friday	Saturday	Sunday
0000–0100							
0100–0200							
0200–0300							
0300–0400							
0400–0500							
0500–0600							
0600–0700							
0700–0800							
0800–0900							
0900–1000							

	Monday	Tuesday	Wednesday	Thursday	Friday	Saturday	Sunday
1000–1100							
1100–1200							
1300–1400							
1400–1500							
1500–1600							
1600–1700							
1700–1800							
1800–1900							
1900–2000							
2000–2100							
2100–2200							
2200–2300							
2300–2400							

Evaluating my activity diary

Answer the following questions to help you evaluate your activities this week.

What patterns did I notice from my diary?	
Was there anything which surprised me?	
When am I most active and how do I feel at these times?	
When am I least active and how do I feel at these times?	
When am I feeling worst and what am I doing at these times?	
Are there things which I'm doing a lot but which aren't giving me pleasure or satisfaction?	
When am I feeling the most amount of pleasure? What am I doing?	
When am I feeling the most amount of achievement? What am I doing?	
How much of a range of activities am I doing?	
Which things am I doing that I want to do more of?	
Which things am I doing that I want to do less of?	
What could I do at those times when I feel worst?	
Are there things which I want to start doing again?	
Other comments:	
What have I learned? How can I use what you've learned? What will I do?	

Finding activities that give me pleasure and a sense of achievement

It can be useful to build up a list of activities which are likely to lift your mood. You can use this list like a menu and pick activities from it in order to plan your week or day or pick activities from it to do when you feel at a loss about what to do.

What activities give me pleasure?	
What activities used to give me pleasure?	
What activities give me a sense of achievement?	
What activities used to give me a sense of achievement?	
What activities do/did I do with others?	
What activities do others do which I'd like to try?	
What activities do/did I do alone?	
What physical activities do/did I do?	
What mental activities do/did I do?	
What activities do/did I do outside the house?	
What activities do/did I do which take just 5–10 minutes?	
What activities do/did I do which relax me?	
What activities am I interested in but have never tried?	

Predicting pleasure and a sense of achievement

Before doing an activity predict how much pleasure and sense of achievement you will get from doing it. Notice at the time of doing the activity how much pleasure and achievement you actually felt and record this.

Activity	Predicted pleasure (0–10)	Predicted achievement (0–10)	Actual pleasure (0–10)	Actual achievement (0–10)	Comments

What patterns did I notice?

What have I learned? How can I use what you've learned? What will I do?

Doing things step-by-step

In order to make activities more manageable, they can be divided up into a list of smaller steps. Pick an activity which at the moment feels difficult and overwhelming and which you therefore might have been putting off doing. List the steps needed to complete this task. As you complete the steps put a tick next to them.

Activity:	

Step number	What I will do	What assistance and/or resources I might need	When I will do it

Did I manage to complete all the steps?
If not, why might that be and what could I do about it?
If I completed all the steps what was it like?
What have I learned? How can I use what I've learned? What will I do?

Evaluating thoughts which make me less active

Some thoughts can make you less likely to engage in activities, for example, 'I won't enjoy it' or 'It's too difficult'. Identify what thoughts you have which make it less likely that you will engage in activities. Use the *Evaluating my thoughts* and *Evaluating my thought distortions* worksheets to come up with alternative, more helpful thoughts. Look over these alternative thoughts when you next have one of the unhelpful thoughts.

Thought which makes me less active	Alternative, helpful thought

Which alternative thoughts have been most helpful? Put an asterix (*) next to them.

Chapter 4
Anxiety

Worksheet summaries

Chapter 4.1 Anxiety

The following worksheets are used to increase clients' and therapists' understanding of the clients' anxiety and fears: *Drawing out my experiences of anxiety, My experiences of anxiety, Analysing my fear, Identifying my safety behaviours* and *Listing my safety behaviours*.

Drawing out my experiences of anxiety

Clients can use this worksheet to identify their thoughts, feelings, physical sensations and behaviours which maintain their feelings of anxiety. Particular types of thinking distortions associated with anxiety are considered, for example, overestimating danger and awfulness and underestimating coping and help.

My experiences of anxiety

Clients can use this checklist to help them consider whether their experiences are typical of anxiety as well as to identify whether such experiences have happened in the past and/or now.

Analysing my fear

This worksheet helps clients to analyse those factors which increase or decrease a particular fear.

The following worksheets are used to assist clients in changing their experiences of anxiety: *Evaluating my fear, Evaluating the probability of my fears, Imagining the worst, Exposing myself to situations I fear, Experimenting with my safety behaviours* and *Practising relaxation*.

Evaluating my fear

Clients can use this worksheet to evaluate how they perceive the four aspects of the anxiety equation: likelihood, awfulness, coping and the situation.

Evaluating the probability of my fears

Clients may feel less anxious if they come to believe that a feared outcome is less likely than they initially thought. This worksheet suggests various ways to do this, for example, researching statistics, using past experiences and analysing the probability of a chain of events.

Imagining the worst

Clients may try to avoid imagining their worst fears and so may benefit from imagining their worst fear sufficiently long enough for their associated feelings of anxiety to reduce. They can repeat this process and record their experiences on this worksheet.

Exposing myself to situations I fear

When clients intend to go into particular situations which they fear they may find it helpful to record how their level of anxiety changes over time. They may use this worksheet in conjunction with the *Drawing up a ladder of behaviours* and the *Working my way up the ladder of behaviours* worksheets.

Identifying my safety behaviours

The type of safety behaviour which a client uses will be related to what feared catastrophe they are trying to prevent. This worksheet lists some common fears and associated safety behaviours in order to help clients identify theirs.

Listing my safety behaviours

Clients can list all of their safety behaviours and link them to how they hope they'll help, that is, what feared catastrophe they use them to try to prevent.

Experimenting with my safety behaviours

Clients may learn about the effects, advantages and disadvantages of their safety behaviours by comparing and contrasting two scenarios: one in which they use all of their safety behaviours as far as they can and one in which they try not to use any safety behaviours as far as they can.

Practising relaxation

Keeping a diary of their relaxation practice using this worksheet may help clients in a number of ways, for example, noticing how often and for how long they are practising relaxation and noticing whether and when the practice is affecting their feelings of anxiety. They can then plan their practice for the future.

Chapter 4.2 Panic

My experiences of panic

Clients can use this checklist to help them consider whether their experiences are typical of panic as well as to identify whether such experiences have happened in the past and/or now.

Recording my experiences of panic

Clients can keep a diary of their experiences of panic in order to begin to analyse various factors which affect it, for example, situations, physical sensations, thoughts and coping strategies.

Identifying my fears which lead me to panic

During experiences of panic, clients' fears are likely to be linked to particular physical sensations; for example, a racing heart may be experienced as evidence of a heart attack. This worksheet lists some common physical sensations of anxiety and associated fears. The benefits of completing this worksheet could include: identifying fears, making the link between fears and physical sensations and discovering that others have previously interpreted their physical sensations in a similar way.

Testing out my physical sensations of anxiety

Once clients have identified what fear they associate with which physical sensation, client and therapist can work together to devise an experiment to test out their assumption. It is hoped that clients may learn that their physical sensations are not evidence of their worst fear; for example, a racing heart is not evidence of a heart attack.

It is important to consider how any ongoing health problems might impact on these experiments; for example, if the client has an underlying health problem it may be important to get the all-clear from the client's GP before continuing with the experiment.

Chapter 4.3 Worry or generalised anxiety disorder (GAD)

My experiences of worry

Clients can use this checklist to help them consider whether their experiences are typical of worry as well as to identify whether such experiences have happened in the past and/or now.

Recording worry for one day / one week

It can be helpful for clients to notice how often and in what situations they are worrying. They can choose whether to keep a diary of their worrying for one day or for one week. The purpose of the diaries is not to capture the content of the worry but rather to notice each time it happens. They can then begin to explore patterns in their worry and links with their mood.

Understanding why I worry

This worksheet lists some common beliefs about the usefulness of worry (positive beliefs about worry) and beliefs about the negative consequences of worry (negative beliefs about worry). Clients can rate all the beliefs from 0–100% according to how much they believe them and therefore identify which beliefs they hold most strongly. They can also identify other positive and negative beliefs they hold about worry and rate their conviction in them from 0%–100%.

Deciding what to do about my worries

This worksheet helps clients to consider what their worry is about and therefore what approach may be the most helpful one. The two main strategies suggested are: problem-solving for worries when there is something helpful the client may be able to do about it and distraction when there isn't. For each strategy clients are directed towards the relevant worksheet.

Planning time to worry

For those clients where planned worry time may be helpful, they can use this worksheet to schedule worry time and to observe what happened and how they felt.

How realistic are my worries?

This worksheet can be used by clients to evaluate whether their worries actually happen. They can also notice any themes in their worries.

Learning to tolerate uncertainty

This worksheet can be used with clients who find it difficult to tolerate uncertainty. Clients are required to identify situations where there is uncertainty, to order these and to enter into them in order to evaluate what happens when they begin to go into more situations where there is uncertainty. It may be that they also increasingly reduce their safety behaviours as a way of learning to tolerate uncertainty.

Chapter 4.4   Obsessive compulsive disorder (OCD)

My experiences of obsessive-compulsive disorder

Clients can use this checklist to help them consider whether their experiences are typical of OCD as well as to identify whether such experiences have happened in the past and/or now.

Recording my obsessions and compulsions

This worksheet can be used by clients to help them to notice more their experiences of OCD and to break them down into components which are likely to form part of a cognitive behavioural formulation. Therapists will need to ensure that clients understand what these components mean.

Recording a compulsion for one day / one week

Clients can begin to notice how often and at what times they carry out compulsions. This may help them begin to notice patterns which can then be explored in order to aid the understanding of the client's difficulty. Clients can choose to do this over one day or one week.

Identifying my fears about thoughts

This worksheet lists some common beliefs about thoughts which may lead to experiences of OCD. Clients rate all of these beliefs from 0%–100% according to how much they believe them and therefore identify which beliefs they hold most strongly.

Evaluating explanations for my difficulties – OCD

This worksheet can be used to help those clients who have an understanding of their intrusive thoughts which perpetuates their experiences of OCD; for example, 'Having these thoughts means that I'm a bad person and that I want to act on them.' Clients may want to use the beliefs identified in the worksheet *Identifying my fears about thoughts*. Therapists help clients to identify an alternative explanation for their intrusive thoughts: one which may help clients to feel less compelled to engage in neutralising strategies. Over time they can build up evidence for these two explanations.

Exposing myself to my intrusive thoughts

For some clients it may be helpful for them to carry out exposure work to their intrusive thoughts. This worksheet helps clients to record their experiences during the exposure and focuses on changes in their degree of anxiety over time. This may help clients to notice various things, for example, whether they are carrying out exposure for long enough and how anxious they feel at each stage of the process.

Testing out whether thoughts can cause things to happen

This worksheet can be used with clients who believe that having certain thoughts means that the thoughts will come true. Clients identify a series of behavioural experiments whereby they purposefully have a thought, predict how likely they think it is to happen and then notice whether it does happen.

Recording changes in my compulsions

As clients work towards reducing their compulsions they can use this worksheet to record their experiences. A measure of anxiety before and after their compulsions is included in order to notice any changes (or lack of).

Recording situations when I don't neutralise

This worksheet can be used by clients to keep a record of when they don't neutralise.

Chapter 4.5   Health anxiety

My experiences of health anxiety

Clients can use this checklist to help them consider whether their experiences are typical of health anxiety as well as to identify whether such experiences have happened in the past and/or now.

Finding alternative explanations for physical sensations

This worksheet can be used when clients tend to interpret physical sensations as indicating serious health problems, for example, a headache is interpreted as evidence for a tumour. Clients consider other explanations for their physical sensations and assign % likelihoods, eg dehydration (40%), insufficient sleep (20%), a virus (20%), eye strain (5%), a reaction to certain food or drink (5%), a tumour (10%). They can also draw the percentage on a pie chart, for example:

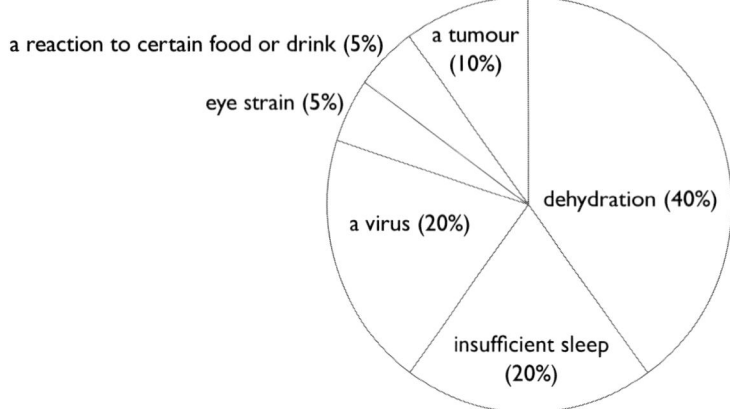

Doing this exercise may mean that their original explanation, for example, a tumour, is seen as a less likely explanation for their physical sensation.

Evaluating the likely seriousness of physical sensations

This worksheet can help clients to evaluate how likely it is that a particular physical sensation indicates a serious physical health condition. Clients consider how many people might have such a sensation at that time, for example, 100 out of 1000 people might have a headache. They go on to consider other scenarios which are increasingly less likely, for example, 1 out of 1000 people might find out that their headaches indicate something medically serious. This may help clients to discover that the worst-case scenario is less likely than they expect.

Evaluating explanations for my difficulties – health anxiety

This worksheet can be used to help those clients who have an understanding of their experiences which perpetuates their health anxiety, for example, 'Having these physical sensations means that I have a serious illness.' Therapists help clients to identify an alternative explanation for their experiences: one which may help clients to feel less anxious about their health. Over time they can build up evidence for these two explanations.

Chapter 4.6 Social anxiety

My experiences of social anxiety

Clients can use this checklist to help them consider whether their experiences are typical of social anxiety as well as to identify whether such experiences have happened in the past and/or now.

Recording social situations

This worksheet can be used by clients after they have been in social situations in order to reflect on the objective evidence about what happened. It reminds clients to use objective evidence to evaluate a social situation rather than their feelings of anxiety.

Evaluating my thoughts in social situations

This worksheet extends the work started in *Recording social situations*. It can be used by clients to evaluate their thoughts about social situations and can be used in conjunction with other worksheets for evaluating thoughts, such as: *Evaluating my thoughts – helpful questions, Evaluating my thoughts – my favourite questions, Thought distortions, Noticing my thought distortions* and *Evaluating my thought distortions – helpful questions*.

Experimenting with focusing on myself

Often clients who experience social anxiety will focus a lot on themselves and their 'performance'. This worksheet is to be used in conjunction with a behavioural experiment carried out in a session. The behavioural experiment involves therapist and client holding two conversations: one in which the client uses self-focus and other safety behaviours and one in which the client tries to reduce their self-focus and safety behaviours. Client and therapist can then reflect on their experiences.

Using video or audio feedback

This worksheet may help clients prepare for and reflect on behavioural experiments involving video or audio feedback. The behavioural experiment is likely to involve a social situation in which particular predictions clients make, for example, 'I will blush', can be recorded and evaluated objectively, for example, by predicting and recording the colour of the client's skin.

Chapter 4.7 Post-traumatic stress disorder (PTSD)

My experiences after trauma

Clients can use this checklist to help them consider whether their experiences are typical of PTSD as well as to identify whether such experiences have happened in the past and/or now.

Identifying things that make me remember the trauma

Clients who experience flashbacks to memories of trauma can use this diary to help them to begin to understand whether there are particular aspects of the trauma which they are tending to remember and whether there are particular situations or experiences which are triggers to the flashbacks.

Listing triggers to memories of the trauma

Once clients have identified potential triggers to their memories of trauma, for example, by using the worksheet *Identifying things that make me remember the trauma*, they can order them according to how much distress the triggers lead them to feel.

Grading traumatic memories

Once clients have identified the main aspects of their memories of trauma, for example, by using the worksheet *Identifying things that make me remember the trauma*, they can grade them according to how much distress they feel when recalling them. Clients can also consider what thoughts accompany these memories, both thoughts they had at the time of the trauma and thoughts they have currently.

Managing memories of the trauma

Clients can keep a diary of how they cope with their memories of trauma in order to help them reflect on what are helping coping responses.

Evaluating guilt – helpful questions

Evaluating guilt – my responses

Clients can use these worksheets if they are experiencing guilt about what they did or didn't do in relation to their traumatic experiences. Clients are guided through a series of questions to help them evaluate any thoughts which lead them to feel guilt. They can read the questions in *Evaluating guilt – helpful questions* and write down their responses on *Evaluating guilt – my responses*.

Drawing out my experiences of anxiety

Below is a model of anxiety. Consider how your experiences might fit into this model.

Situation.	In which situations do I typically feel anxious?
Overestimating danger.	What danger do I predict?
Overestimating awfulness.	What is the awful outcome I predict?
Underestimating coping.	How do I predict I'll cope?
Underestimating help.	How do I predict others/the situation will help?
Anxiety/Physical sensations.	How do I feel? How does my body change?
Safety behaviours.	What do I do in order to try to prevent danger?
Avoidance.	What do I avoid in order to try to prevent danger?

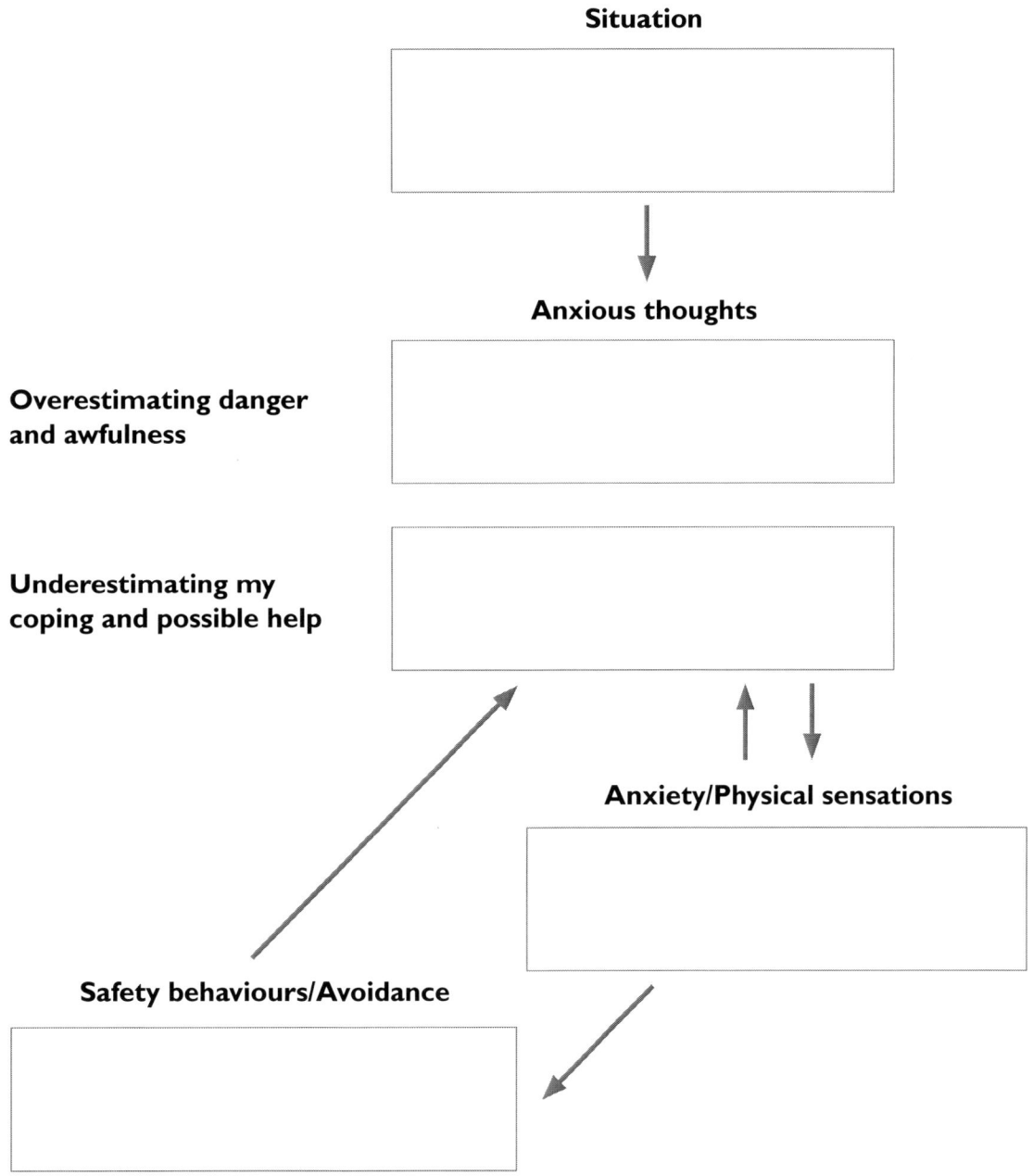

My experiences of anxiety

Below is a list of common experiences for those people suffering from anxiety. Identify which experiences of anxiety you have experienced recently and in the past.

Possible experiences of anxiety	Have I experienced this?	When?	Do I experience this now?	Comments
Feeling anxious	Yes/No		Yes/No	
Feeling fearful	Yes/No		Yes/No	
Feeling worried	Yes/No		Yes/No	
Feeling very irritable	Yes/No		Yes/No	
Heart racing	Yes/No		Yes/No	
Sweating	Yes/No		Yes/No	
'Butterflies' in stomach	Yes/No		Yes/No	
Tensed muscles	Yes/No		Yes/No	
Light-headedness	Yes/No		Yes/No	
Nausea	Yes/No		Yes/No	
Dizziness	Yes/No		Yes/No	
Tingling in hands/feet/arms	Yes/No		Yes/No	
Trembling	Yes/No		Yes/No	
Fidgeting a lot	Yes/No		Yes/No	
Quick and shallow breathing	Yes/No		Yes/No	
Expecting problems or the worst to happen	Yes/No		Yes/No	
Thinking that problems are impossible to solve	Yes/No		Yes/No	
Thinking that I can't cope	Yes/No		Yes/No	
Focused thinking on fears	Yes/No		Yes/No	
Difficulties in problem solving	Yes/No		Yes/No	

Analysing my fear

Use the following questions to help you understand better one of your fears.

What is my fear?
Are there times of day that make it better or worse?
Are there certain places or aspects of the situation that make it worse or better?
Does having other people around make it better or worse? If so, which people?
Are there certain things about me that make it better or worse, for example, level of tiredness, feeling excited, feeling hot?
What other things make it worse or better?
What have I learned? How can I use what I've learned? What will I do?

Evaluating my fear

👥 Use the questions below to evaluate four aspects of your fear.

What is my fear?	

The likelihood of my fear

1. Is there anything to suggest that my fear is less likely to occur than I think?
2. Looking at it objectively how likely is my fear?

How awful it would be if my fear happened

3. If my fear did happen how might it not be as awful as I expect it to be?

My ability to cope

4. Is there anything to suggest that I'd cope better than I expect?
5. If my fear did happen how would I cope?
6. How have I coped before in this or similar situations?

Helpful aspects of the situation

7. Is there anything about the situation that could be helpful to me?

How would I summarise all of this information?
What have I learned? How can I use what I've learned? What will I do?

Evaluating the probability of my fears

What is my fear?	
How likely do I think it is that it will happen?	% likely
How can I find out how likely it might be, for example, find out statistics, test it out?	
What did I find out from my research/tests?	
What have been my experiences of my fear happening to date?	
Based on these experiences, how likely does it seem that my fear will happen?	% likely
If my fear is a sequence of events:	
What is the first step and how likely is it?	%
What is the second step and how likely is it?	%
What is the third step and how likely is it?	%
What is the fourth step and how likely is it?	%
What is the fifth step and how likely is it?	%
What is the overall likelihood? Multiply all the percentages, that is, first % x second % x third %, etc.	%
What have I learned about how likely it is that my fear will happen?	
What have I learned? How can I use what I've learned? What will I do?	

Imagining the worst

Spending time thinking about our worst fears can sometimes be helpful. Identify what your worst fear is, plan to spend some time imagining it happening and see how anxious and upset you feel over time. Do things change?

My worst fear	Amount of time spent imagining it	How anxious or upset I felt (0–10)	What I learned

What happened when I spent time imagining my worst fear?
Did how distressed I felt change over time?
What have I learned? How can I use what I've learned? What will I do?

Exposing myself to situations I fear

Make a note of every time you go into a situation which you fear. Record your level of anxiety before, during and after the event.

Date	Feared situation	Anxiety before (0–10)	Anxiety during (0–10)	Anxiety after (0–10)	Comments

What happened during my exposure sessions?
What have I learned? How can I use what I've learned? What will I do?

Identifying my safety behaviours

Below are some common fears and possible associated safety behaviours. Note down what safety behaviours you have used in the past and what safety behaviours you continue to use now.

Fear	Safety behaviour	Have I used it in the past?	Do I use it now?
Having a heart attack	Deep slow breaths		
	Sit down		
	Go to A&E or call 999		
	Other		
Fainting	Deep slow breaths		
	Sit down		
	Have a drink of water		
	Other		
Vomiting	Go to the toilet		
	Get fresh air		
	Have a mint		
	Have a drink of water		
	Leave the situation		
	Other		
Losing control of my thoughts	Try to control my thoughts		
	Try to avoid certain thoughts		
	Other		
Losing control of my behaviour	Focus on what I'm doing		
	Avoid certain places		
	Other		
Stopping breathing	Take deep breaths		
	Focus on breathing		
	Other		
Making the wrong decision	Ask others for reassurance		
	Don't make a decision		
	Other		
Not coping alone	Don't go out alone		
	Other		
Other fear			

Listing my safety behaviours

👥 As you identify your safety behaviours note them down and work out what feared event you hope they will prevent from happening.

Safety behaviour	How I think it might prevent something bad from happening

Are there any themes or patterns to my safety behaviours?

What have I learned? How can I use what I've learned? What will I do?

Experimenting with my safety behaviours

👥 In the same situation try out two different ways of being. First of all try to decide how long you might do this for. In the first occasion try to use all of your safety behaviours as far as you can; Then, still in the same situation, try not to use any safety behaviours as far as you can. If possible, get feedback from others in the situation about how they thought it went. Answer the following questions to see how the two were different.

1 – Using my safety behaviours

How anxious did I feel out of 10?	
How did it go? What was it like for me and what was it like for anybody else who can give me feedback?	

2 – Dropping my safety behaviours

How anxious did I feel out of 10?	
How did it go? What was it like for me and what was it like for anybody else who can give me feedback?	

Comparing the two

During which scenario did I feel better and why?
Which scenario did others rate as better and why?
What was different between the two?
What did I learn from this experiment that could be helpful in the future?
What have I learned? How can I use what I've learned? What will I do?

Practising relaxation

Every time you practise relaxation make a note of the following things.

Date	Length of practice	Type of relaxation	Anxiety before (0–10)	Anxiety after (0–10)	Comments

What have I noticed about practising relaxation?
Were there things which made it easier or harder to do?
What will I carry on doing? How will I overcome obstacles?

My experiences of panic

Below is a list of common experiences for those people suffering from panic. Identify which experiences of panic you have experienced recently and in the past.

Possible experiences of anxiety	Have I experienced this?	When?	Do I experience this now?	Comments
Heart racing	Yes/No		Yes/No	
Sweating	Yes/No		Yes/No	
Trembling	Yes/No		Yes/No	
Feeling short of breath	Yes/No		Yes/No	
Chest pain or discomfort	Yes/No		Yes/No	
Nausea	Yes/No		Yes/No	
Feeling dizzy or faint	Yes/No		Yes/No	
Feelings of unreality	Yes/No		Yes/No	
Fear of losing control or of going crazy	Yes/No		Yes/No	
Fear of dying	Yes/No		Yes/No	
Numbness or tingling	Yes/No		Yes/No	
Chills or hot flushes	Yes/No		Yes/No	
Fear of panic attacks	Yes/No		Yes/No	
Fear of the consequences of panic attacks	Yes/No		Yes/No	
Fear of not being able to escape	Yes/No		Yes/No	
Changes in behaviour because of panic	Yes/No		Yes/No	

Recording my experiences of panic

Making a note of your experiences of panic may help you understand better what is happening at those times.

Date	Situation	Anxiety (0–10)	Physical sensations	Thoughts about the sensations	Coping behaviour

What patterns did I notice?
What physical sensations was I having when I felt most anxious?
What thoughts did I have about those physical sensations?
What was the effect of my coping strategies?

Identifying my fears which lead me to panic

Below are some common fears of physical sensations. Work out which ones apply to you and how strongly you believe them *when you feel anxious*. Use the extra boxes to add in any other sensations and fears which you have.

Physical sensation	Fear/Thought	Do I have this fear?	How much do I believe it? (0%–100%)
A feeling of tenseness in the chest muscles A racing heart	I'm having a heart attack.	Yes/No	%
Changes in breathing	I can't breathe.	Yes/No	%
	I'm going to pass out.	Yes/No	%
Dizziness/light-headedness	I'm going to collapse.	Yes/No	%
Numbness or tingling	I'm having a stroke.	Yes/No	%
Difficulty in concentrating or thinking clearly	I'm going mad.	Yes/No	%
Feelings of unreality	I'm going to lose control.	Yes/No	%
Nausea	I'm going to vomit.	Yes/No	%
		Yes/No	%
		Yes/No	%

Testing out my physical sensations of anxiety

👥 Once you have identified which physical sensations of panic you fear, then you can test out your fears. Work with your therapist to think about how you can induce some of these sensations, for example, running up stairs to get your heart racing. Then follow these steps.

Preparing for the experiment

Physical sensations:	
I fear that these sensations mean:	
I believe this:	%
Ways of inducing these sensations:	
What we/I will do when I am having these sensations:	
My prediction for what will happen:	
I believe this:	%
An alternative prediction for what will happen is:	
I believe this:	%

Carrying it out

What did we/I do?	
What happened?	

Reflections

How does this relate to my predictions?	
How much do I now believe my original prediction?	%
How much do I now believe my alternative prediction?	%
What have I learned? How can I use what I've learned? What will I do?	

My experiences of worry

Below is a list of common experiences for those people suffering from worry. Identify which experiences of worry you have experienced recently and in the past.

Possible experiences of worry	Have I experienced this?	When?	Do I experience this now?	Comments
Often worrying	Yes/No		Yes/No	
Worrying about lots of different things	Yes/No		Yes/No	
Often feeling anxious	Yes/No		Yes/No	
Difficulty controlling my worrying	Yes/No		Yes/No	
Often feeling wound-up, tense or restless	Yes/No		Yes/No	
Becoming easily tired and/or worn out	Yes/No		Yes/No	
Having difficulty concentrating	Yes/No		Yes/No	
Often feeling irritable	Yes/No		Yes/No	
Muscles often feeling tense	Yes/No		Yes/No	
Difficulty sleeping	Yes/No		Yes/No	
Worrying interfering with my everyday life	Yes/No		Yes/No	

Recording worry for one day

In order to help you to begin to step back from your worry it can be helpful to notice how often it is happening. Keep a tally chart, where, for example, IIII = 4, of how many times you get caught up in worry over one day, dividing the day up into chunks of one hour.

Date: _____

Morning	Afternoon	Evening	Night-time
0600–0700	1200–1300	1800–1900	0000–0100
0700–0800	1300–1400	1900–2000	0100–0200
0800–0900	1400–1500	2000–2100	0200–0300
0900–1000	1500–1600	2100–2200	0300–0400
1000–1100	1600–1700	2200–2300	0400–0500
1100–1200	1700–1800	2300–2400	0500–0600

When did I worry the *most*?	
Do I know why? What was happening at the time?	
How did I feel at these times?	
When did I worry the *least*?	
Do I know why? What was happening at the time?	
How did I feel at these times?	
Is there anything else that I've learned?	

What have I learned? How can I make use of what I've learned? What will I do?

Recording worry for one week

In order to help you to begin to step back from your worry it can be helpful to notice how often it is happening. Keep a tally chart, where, for example, IIII = 4, of how many times you get caught up in worry over one week.

Week starting: _____

	Morning	**Afternoon**	**Evening**	**Night-time**
Monday				
Tuesday				
Wednesday				
Thursday				
Friday				
Saturday				
Sunday				

When did I worry the *most*?	
Do I know why? What was happening at the time?	
How did I feel at these times?	
When did I worry the *least*?	
Do I know why? What was happening at the time?	
How did I feel at these times?	
Is there anything else that I've learned?	

What have I learned? How can I make use of what I've learned? What will I do?

Understanding why I worry

If you worry a lot, then it is likely that you believe it is in some way a useful strategy. However, you might also think that there are negative things about worry. See how much you agree with the following statements about worry and add any of your own.

Positive beliefs about worry	How much I believe it
If I worry, then I won't be taken by surprise	%
If I worry, then I'll be more prepared for things	%
If I worry, then bad things are less likely to happen	%
If I worry, then I'm more likely to find a solution to a problem	%
If I worry, then I'm a caring and considerate person	%
If I worry, then I don't have to think about worse things	%
If I worry, then	%
If I worry, then	%

Negative beliefs about worry	How much I believe it
If I worry too much, I'll lose control of my mind	%
If I worry too much, I'll feel really bad	%
If I worry too much, it takes up lots of time	%
If I worry too much, it uses up lots of my energy	%
If I worry too much, I'm not good at problem solving	%
If I worry too much, then	%
If I worry too much, then	%

Deciding what to do about my worries

Use the following questions to help you decide what to do about your worries.

What is my worry?
Is there a very low probability of it happening?
Is there anything helpful and practical I can do about what I fear might happen?
Do I have any control over what I fear may happen?
If yes, can I make an action plan for what to do, for example, using the *Solving problems* worksheet?
If there isn't anything helpful I can do about this, how can I distract myself, for example, using the *Distracting myself* worksheet?
What have I learned? How can I use what I've learned? What will I do?

Planning time to worry

Planning in time to worry can have a number of benefits, for example, allowing you to evaluate the usefulness of worry and helping you understand better what you worry about and how you worry. You might benefit from planning an enjoyable and distracting activity for after your worry time. Also it's probably best not to plan to worry just before you go to sleep.

Date	Time when I planned to worry	Time when I worried	What were my experiences?	How did I feel?

What have I learned? How can I use what I've learned? What will I do?

How realistic are my worries?

It can be helpful to keep a diary of your worries in order to be able to evaluate how realistic or likely they are. Note down what your worry or prediction is, for example, 'I'll lose my job' and when you think it will happen by, for example, 'Within the next month'. After that time frame has passed, evaluate whether or not your prediction came true, for example, 'I had a review at work and was told I was doing well, and so kept my job'.

Worry/Prediction and time frame	What actually happened

Are there any themes to my worries?
How accurate have my predictions been?
What have I learned? How can I use what I've learned? What will I do?

Learning to tolerate uncertainty

It can be helpful to learn to think differently when there is uncertainty in a situation, that is, when you can't predict what will happen. In order to do this, work out a range of situations in which there will be uncertainty. Put these situations in order of how anxious you imagine you would feel in them. Practise going into these situations, starting with the easiest first, and notice what happens. You might also want to use the *How realistic are my worries?* worksheet.

Situation	How anxious I might be (0–10)	What happened	What I learned

What happened?

What have I learned? How can I use what I've learned? What will I do?

My experiences of obsessive-compulsive disorder

👥 Below is a list of common experiences for people suffering from obsessive-compulsive disorder (OCD). Identify which experiences of OCD you have experienced recently and in the past.

Possible experiences of OCD	Have I experienced this?	When?	Do I experience this now?	Comments
Thoughts which I think I must act on	Yes/No		Yes/No	
Thoughts which I think I shouldn't have	Yes/No		Yes/No	
Thoughts of events which I think will then happen	Yes/No		Yes/No	
Thoughts which I think mean something bad about me	Yes/No		Yes/No	
Thoughts which mean I feel very anxious/ distressed	Yes/No		Yes/No	
Feeling compelled to do things because of thoughts	Yes/No		Yes/No	
Feeling compelled to repeat certain actions	Yes/No		Yes/No	
Trying to suppress or avoid certain thoughts	Yes/No		Yes/No	

Recording my obsessions and compulsions

👥 Make a note of every time you have an intrusive thought and/or compulsion.

Date	Situation	Emotions (0–10)	Intrusive thought	Interpretation of thought	Compulsive behaviour

What patterns did I notice?

Recording a compulsion for one day

Keep a record of the times you engage in one of your compulsions over one day, dividing the day up into chunks of one hour. Either record how many times you do the compulsion in the form of a tally chart, where, for example, IIII = 4, or record the length of time you spent carrying out the compulsion, for example, 4 minutes.

Compulsion: _____

Date: _____

Morning	Afternoon	Evening	Night-time
0600–0700	1200–1300	1800–1900	0000–0100
0700–0800	1300–1400	1900–2000	0100–0200
0800–0900	1400–1500	2000–2100	0200–0300
0900–1000	1500–1600	2100–2200	0300–0400
1000–1100	1600–1700	2200–2300	0400–0500
1100–1200	1700–1800	2300–2400	0500–0600

What patterns did I notice about my compulsion?

Is there anything else that I've learned?

What have I learned? How can I make use of what I've learned? What will I do?

Recording a compulsion for one week

Keep a record of the times you engage in one of your compulsions over one week. Either record how many times you do the compulsion in the form of a tally chart, where, for example, IIII = 4, or record the length of time you spent carrying out the compulsion, for example, 4 minutes.

Compulsion:

Week starting:

	Morning	Afternoon	Evening	Night-time
Monday				
Tuesday				
Wednesday				
Thursday				
Friday				
Saturday				
Sunday				

What patterns did I notice about my compulsion?

Is there anything else that I've learned?

What have I learned? How can I make use of what I've learned? What will I do?

Identifying my fears about thoughts

Below are some common fears about thoughts. Work out which ones apply to you and how strongly you believe them *when you feel anxious*. Add in any other fears you have about particular thoughts.

Date: _____

Fear/Thought	Do I have this fear?	How much do I believe it (0%–100%)
I shouldn't be having these kinds of thoughts	Yes/No	%
These thoughts mean that I'm a bad person	Yes/No	%
Having these thoughts means that I want them to happen	Yes/No	%
These thoughts mean that they're likely to happen unless I do something to stop it	Yes/No	%
I am responsible for making sure that these thoughts don't come true	Yes/No	%
I need to get control over my thoughts, otherwise they will or might go out of control	Yes/No	%
Other fear		%

Re-rate how much you believe these statements every few weeks to see if they are changing. What do you notice?

Evaluating explanations for my difficulties – OCD

👥 Identify both your original explanation for your difficulties, for example, 'Having these thoughts means I'm a bad person', as well as an alternative explanation, for example, 'I might have certain thoughts because I'm a kind person who doesn't want them to happen'. Write these two alternative explanations in the appropriate columns below. Find and evaluate the evidence you use to support these two explanations.

Evidence for my original explanation	Evidence for my alternative explanation

Which explanation does the evidence support best?

What have I learned? How can I use what I've learned? What will I do?

Exposing myself to my intrusive thoughts

👥 Work with your therapist to identify some of your intrusive thoughts which you feel able to expose yourself to. Record the details of exposing yourself to one such thought below.

Intrusive thought:	

Date	Length of exposure to intrusive thought	Anxiety before (0–10)	Anxiety during (0–10)	Anxiety after (0–10)	Comments

What happened during my exposure sessions?

What have I learned? How can I use what I've learned? What will I do?

Testing out whether thoughts can cause things to happen

👥 You might think that having certain thoughts will mean they will happen or that having certain thoughts about doing something will mean you will do it. Work out a list of such thoughts and rate how likely you think they are to happen and how anxious you feel when you have them. Include positive thoughts. Starting with the thought that makes you feel least anxious, practise having the thought without neutralising it in any way. See what happens.

I believe that having certain thoughts means that:

I believe this:	%

Thought	How likely I think it is to happen (0%–100%)	Anxiety (0–10)	What happened when I had this thought

What happened when I tested out having these thoughts?

How much do I now believe my original belief?	%

What have I learned? How can I use what I've learned? What will I do?

Recording changes in my compulsions

As you aim to reduce your compulsions, for example, time spent washing and/or number of times you check something, make a note of the following.

Date	Situation	Compulsion	Duration or frequency of compulsion	Anxiety before (0–10)	Anxiety after (0–10)

What happened when I reduced my compulsions?

What have I learned? How can I use what I've learned? What will I do?

Recording situations when I don't neutralise

Draw up a list of situations in which you could expose yourself to your intrusive thoughts and fears and then not use any of your neutralising strategies. Make a note of your experiences.

Feared situation/ action	Estimated anxiety (0–10)	Anxiety during (0–10)	Anxiety after (0–10)	Comments

What happened when I exposed myself to feared situations?

What have I learned? How can I use what I've learned? What will I do?

My experiences of health anxiety

Below is a list of common experiences for those people suffering from health anxiety. Identify which experiences of health anxiety you have experienced recently and in the past.

Possible experiences of health anxiety	Have I experienced this?	When?	Do I experience this now?	Comments
Frequent worry about my health	Yes/No		Yes/No	
Often feeling unwell	Yes/No		Yes/No	
Often feeling anxious	Yes/No		Yes/No	
Intense fear of having a serious health condition	Yes/No		Yes/No	
Believing that I have a serious health condition	Yes/No		Yes/No	
Interpreting physical sensations as evidence of a serious health condition	Yes/No		Yes/No	
Often seeking medical advice	Yes/No		Yes/No	
In the long term not feeling reassured by medical advice	Yes/No		Yes/No	
Asking others for reassurance about my health	Yes/No		Yes/No	
Often conducting research into serious health conditions	Yes/No		Yes/No	
Avoiding information about serious health conditions	Yes/No		Yes/No	
Often checking my body for indications of a serious health condition	Yes/No		Yes/No	
Health fears interfearing with everyday life	Yes/No		Yes/No	

Finding alternative explanations for physical sensations

Identify a physical sensation which you think suggests that you have a serious health problem. Use the following questions to consider other possible explanations for the physical sensation.

| My physical sensation(s): | |

What are the possible explanations for this sensation and how likely is each explanation? Combining all the likelihoods together should add up to 100%.

Possible explanation for the sensation(s)	Likelihood
	%
	%
	%
	%
	%
	%

For each explanation draw a slice of the pie to represent how likely it is.

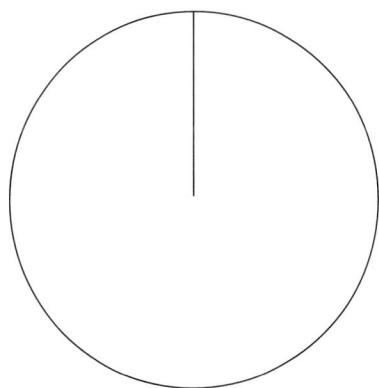

Were the answers what I expected?	
If not, what do I make of that? Why do I think that is?	
Which explanations seem most likely?	
What have I learned? How can I use what I've learned? What will I do?	

Evaluating the likely seriousness of physical sensations

👥 Identify a physical sensation which you think suggests that you have a serious health problem. Use the following questions to estimate over time how many people might then experience the following scenarios.

My physical sensation(s):	

How many people in		might have this sensation today?	
How many people in		might continue to have this sensation tomorrow?	
How many people in		might continue to have this sensation in a week's time?	
How many people in		might continue to have this sensation in a month's time?	
How many people in		might seek medical advice about this sensation?	
How many people in		might find out that it's something medically serious?	
How many people in		might find out that it's something untreatable?	

What have I learned from doing this?

What have I learned? How can I use what I've learned? What will I do?

Evaluating explanations for my difficulties – health anxiety

Identify both your original explanation for your difficulties, for example, 'I have something physically wrong with me', as well as an alternative explanation, for example, 'I worry that I have something physically wrong with me'. Find and evaluate the evidence you use to support these two explanations.

Evidence for my original explanation	Evidence for my alternative explanation

Which explanation does the evidence support best?

What have I learned? How can I use what I've learned? What will I do?

My experiences of social anxiety

Below is a list of common experiences for those people suffering from social anxiety. Identify which experiences of social anxiety you have experienced recently and in the past.

Possible experiences of social anxiety	Have I experienced this?	When?	Do I experience this now?	Comments
Feeling very anxious in social situations	Yes/No		Yes/No	
Feeling very self-conscious in social situations	Yes/No		Yes/No	
Thinking that I'm stupid/no good/boring	Yes/No		Yes/No	
Thinking that I'm inadequate	Yes/No		Yes/No	
Thinking that I'm unlovable	Yes/No		Yes/No	
Thinking that I'm being judged negatively	Yes/No		Yes/No	
Withdrawing in social situations	Yes/No		Yes/No	
Avoiding social situations	Yes/No		Yes/No	
Blushing in social situations	Yes/No		Yes/No	
Sweating in social situations	Yes/No		Yes/No	
Shaking in social situations	Yes/No		Yes/No	

Recording social situations

After a social situation, if you use your feelings to judge how the situation went then this may lead to unhelpful thoughts and accompanying distress. After a social situation, record what happened ensuring that you write down facts rather than feelings.

Date	Social situation	Anxiety (0–10)	What happened? What went well? What are the facts?

What have I learned from keeping this diary?
What have I learned? How can I use what I've learned? What will I do?

Evaluating my thoughts in social situations

Often when people are anxious in social situations they judge the situation using information about how they are feeling. For example, someone who feels shaky and anxious may think that they look anxious and that they are not being interesting even though others would disagree. Use this worksheet to help you find 'evidence' to evaluate your thoughts. The evidence should be both 'internal', from how you are feeling, and 'external', from what is happening around you.

What is the situation?	
How am I feeling (and how strongly out of 10)?	
What am I thinking?	
How much do I believe this thought from 0% to 100%?	
What is the internal evidence which makes me believe this thought?	
What is the external evidence that doesn't support this thought?	
What questions from the *Evaluating my thoughts* and *Evaluating my thought distortions* worksheets are useful for this thought?	
How would I answer these questions?	
What is a balanced conclusion based on all of the evidence?	
How much do I believe this thought from 0% to 100%?	
What have I learned? How can I use what I've learned? What will I do?	

Experimenting with focusing on myself

With your therapist, hold two conversations about any topic, each about two to three minutes long. In the first conversation focus as much as possible on yourself, for example, on what you are saying, how you are coming across and what you might look like. You might also make use of any safety behaviours you normally use in social situations. In the second conversation focus your attention externally as much as possible, that is, on the other person and on what they are saying and try not to use any safety behaviours.

Conversation 1 – Focusing on myself

How anxious did I feel out of 10?	
How self-conscious did I feel out of 10?	
How did the conversation go? What was it like for me and what was it like for my therapist?	

Conversation 2 – Focusing on the other person

How anxious did I feel out of 10?	
How self-conscious did I feel out of 10?	
How did the conversation go? What was it like for me and what was it like for my therapist?	

Comparing the two conversations

During which conversation did I feel better and why?	
Which conversation did my therapist enjoy the most and why?	
What was different between the two conversations?	
What have I learned? How can I use what I've learned? What will I do?	

Using video or audio feedback

👥 With your therapist, set up a scenario in which you can test out some of your social fears using a video or audio recorder. Examples are how much you blush, shake or sweat.

What is the situation? What will I do?
What do I predict I will look/sound like?
Is there a way to measure this objectively?
Are there any likely problems with this experiment? If so, what can I do about them?

👥 Carry out the experiment and then answer the following questions.

What happened?
How did this compare with my original predictions?
What have I learned?
How can I use this information in future social situations?

My experiences after trauma

Below is a list of common experiences for those people suffering from the effects of trauma. Identify which you have experienced recently and in the past.

Possible experiences after trauma	Have I experienced this?	When?	Do I experience this now?	Comments
Feeling anxious	Yes/No		Yes/No	
Feeling ashamed and/or guilty	Yes/No		Yes/No	
Feeling angry	Yes/No		Yes/No	
Feeling detached and/or numb	Yes/No		Yes/No	
Nightmares of the trauma	Yes/No		Yes/No	
Flashbacks of the trauma	Yes/No		Yes/No	
Recurrent thoughts of the trauma	Yes/No		Yes/No	
Acting or feeling as if the trauma is happening again	Yes/No		Yes/No	
Trying to avoid thinking about the trauma	Yes/No		Yes/No	
Not being able to remember aspects of the trauma	Yes/No		Yes/No	
Difficulty sleeping	Yes/No		Yes/No	
Difficulty concentrating	Yes/No		Yes/No	
Being easily startled	Yes/No		Yes/No	

Identifying things that make me remember the trauma

👥 Every time you remember the trauma, for example, in a dream or as a flashback, note down the following things.

Date	What aspect of the trauma did I remember?	Emotions (0–10)	What was happening just before I remembered the trauma? What links the current situations to the trauma?

What aspects of the trauma am I tending to remember?

What aspects of situations are causing me to remember the trauma?

Why are they reminding me of the trauma?

Listing triggers to memories of the trauma

After you have used the *Identifying things that make me remember the trauma* worksheet, write down all the triggers to your traumatic memories in order of the amount of distress they cause you.

Trigger to my traumatic memory	Level of distress (0–10)

How can I use these ideas? What will I do?

Grading traumatic memories

When you remember different aspects of the trauma notice how distressed it makes you feel on a scale from 0 to 10; and also note what thoughts you had at the time of the trauma and what thoughts you have now about that aspect of the trauma.

Aspect of the trauma memory	Level of distress (0–10)	Thoughts at the time of the trauma	Thoughts now about the trauma

Which aspects of the trauma do I find most distressing?
Which aspects of the trauma do I find less distressing?

Managing memories of the trauma

Every time you remember the trauma and are very distressed by it, notice what you did afterwards in order to feel better. Your therapist may have ideas for what types of strategies could help.

Date	Situation	Memory	Coping strategy	How effective was it?

Which seem to be the most unhelpful coping strategies?

Which seem to be the most helpful coping strategies?

What have I learned? How can I use what I've learned? What will I do?

Evaluating guilt – helpful questions

👥 Use the first four questions to clarify which thought you're evaluating and how you're feeling. Write your answers on the following worksheet *Evaluating guilt – my responses*.

- What is my unhelpful thought? How much do I believe this from 0% to 100%?

- What emotions do I feel because of having this thought? How strongly do I feel each of them out of 10?

Now use these questions to help you evaluate your unhelpful thought:

1. Am I blaming myself for things which others aren't blaming me for?

2. What would friends or family members say to me if they knew I was thinking this?

3. Am I using a different standard to judge myself from the standard I use for judging others?

4. What would I say to someone else who had this thought?

5. Am I thinking that I knew the consequences of my actions at the time, when I actually didn't then?

6. Am I thinking that alternative courses of action seemed obvious and positive then, when they weren't necessarily?

7. Am I forgetting the context of the situation and why I did what I did?

8. Am I assigning myself more responsibility than seems reasonable?

9. Am I forgetting other aspects of the situation that/people who contributed to the outcome?

10. Am I thinking that extreme emotional reactions were under my control when they weren't?

11. Am I ready to forgive myself? What would be the advantages and disadvantages?

- How much do I now believe my unhelpful thought from 0% to 100%?

- How strongly do I now feel the accompanying emotions out of 10?

- What conclusions have I reached?

Evaluating guilt – my responses

Read through the questions in the proceeding worksheet *Evaluating guilt – helpful questions*. Choose one unhelpful thought and write down your responses to the questions.

My unhelpful thought:	
How much I believe my thought:	0%–100%
My emotion(s) and how strongly I feel them:	0–10

My responses to the questions:

1	
2	
3	
4	
5	
6	
7	
8	
9	
10	
11	

How much do I now believe the unhelpful thought?	%
How strongly do I now feel the emotions listed above?	/ 10
What conclusions have I reached?	

Chapter 5
Other presenting problems

Worksheet summaries

Chapter 5.1 – Low self-esteem

Drawing out my experiences of low self-esteem

Clients can use this worksheet to identify the thoughts, feelings, physical sensations and behaviours which maintain their low self-esteem. Clients are asked to reflect on issues relevant to low self-esteem, for example, beliefs about self-worth and self-criticism.

My experiences of low self-esteem

Clients can use this checklist to help them consider whether their experiences are typical of low self-esteem as well as to identify whether such experiences have happened in the past and/or now.

Recording self-criticism for one day and recording self-criticism for one week

It can be helpful for clients to notice how often and in what situations they are being self-critical. The purpose of the diaries is not to capture the content of the self-criticism but rather to notice each time it happens. They can then begin to explore patterns in their self-criticism and links with their mood.

Answering self-critical thoughts

For clients who experience a lot of self-critical thoughts it can be helpful to identify more compassionate ways of thinking. This worksheet guides clients through a series of questions designed to elicit more self-compassionate thinking.

Evaluating my self-worth

This worksheet suggests factors which contribute to people's evaluation of their self-worth, for example, their relationships, their work and their interests. Clients can evaluate themselves from 0%–100% on these factors and then reflect on what this may tell them about how they evaluate their self-worth. Therapists may wish to help clients consider if there are cognitive biases affecting their responses, for example, are they rating themselves lower than others would rate them; are there other factors on which they'd rate themselves higher?

Identifying good things about me

This worksheet can be used by clients who may not recognise their good qualities. They are guided through a series of questions which help them consider what might be good about themselves.

Building up evidence of my good points

This worksheet can be used by clients who might benefit from noticing more often the actions that they take which could suggest something good about them. It encourages clients to notice what they do more as well as to reflect more on the meaning of their actions.

Chapter 5.2 – Sleep

Keeping a sleep diary

Clients who experience sleep difficulties can use this worksheet to keep a diary of their experiences. The diary focuses on aspects of their sleep which may be addressed when considering helpful changes.

Analysing my sleep diary

Once clients have kept a regular sleep diary then they can use this worksheet to analyse patterns. This may suggest what could be helpful to change.

Drawing out my experiences of low self-esteem

Work out how your experiences of low self-esteem might fit into the model below.

Early experiences. What early experiences shaped how I think about myself, for example, was I set high standards? Was I punished/neglected?

Beliefs about myself. What beliefs do I hold about my abilities and self-worth? What do I think of myself when I am being self-critical?

Situations. In which situations do I notice my low self-esteem?

Thoughts. What do I tend to think or imagine about myself?

Feelings. How do I tend to feel, for example, anxious, angry, disappointed?

Behaviour. What do I do to cope with my feelings, for example, avoid certain situations, criticise myself, hold myself back?

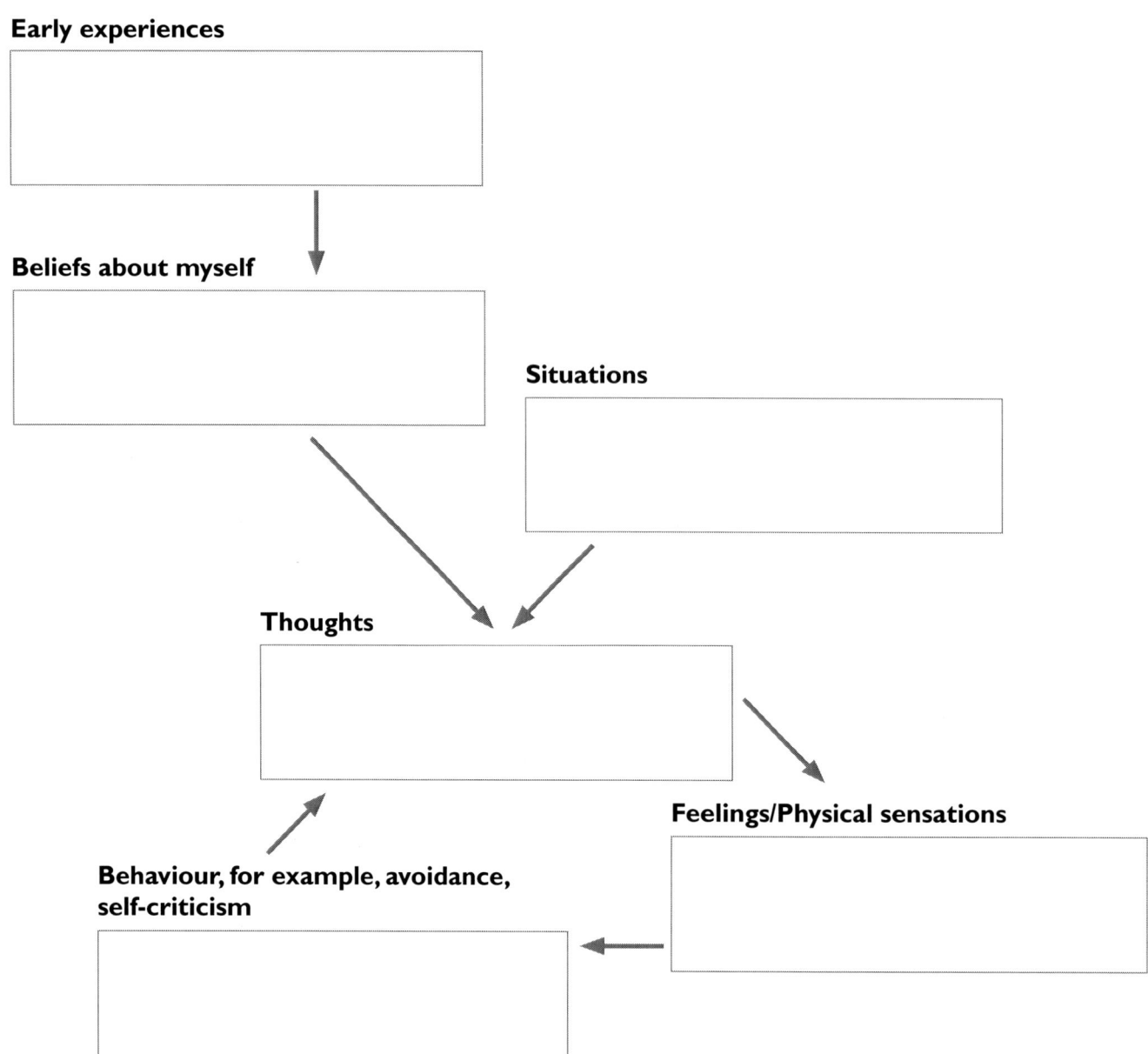

My experiences of low self-esteem

Below is a list of common experiences for those people suffering from low self-esteem. Identify which experiences you have had recently and in the past.

Possible experiences of low self-esteem	Have I experienced this?	When?	Do I experience this now?	Comments
Feeling anxious	Yes/No		Yes/No	
Feeling worried	Yes/No		Yes/No	
Feeling worthless	Yes/No		Yes/No	
Feeling angry at myself	Yes/No		Yes/No	
Feeling demoralised	Yes/No		Yes/No	
Thinking that I can't manage things	Yes/No		Yes/No	
Thinking that things are too difficult for me	Yes/No		Yes/No	
Thinking that I'm not good enough	Yes/No		Yes/No	
A stooped posture	Yes/No		Yes/No	
Avoiding eye contact	Yes/No		Yes/No	
Avoiding new things	Yes/No		Yes/No	
Not putting myself forward	Yes/No		Yes/No	
Asking for reassurance	Yes/No		Yes/No	
Difficulty making decisions	Yes/No		Yes/No	
Criticising myself	Yes/No		Yes/No	

Recording self-criticism for one day

In order to help you to begin to step back from your self-criticism it can be helpful to notice how often it is happening. Keep a tally chart, where, for example, IIII = 4, of how many times you get caught up in self-criticism over one day, dividing the day up into chunks of one hour.

Date:

Morning	Afternoon	Evening	Night-time
0600–0700	1200–1300	1800–1900	0000–0100
0700–0800	1300–1400	1900–2000	0100–0200
0800–0900	1400–1500	2000–2100	0200–0300
0900–1000	1500–1600	2100–2200	0300–0400
1000–1100	1600–1700	2200–2300	0400–0500
1100–1200	1700–1800	2300–2400	0500–0600

When did I have the *most* self-critical thoughts?	
Do I know why? What was happening at the time?	
How did I feel at these times?	
When did I have the *fewest* self-critical thoughts?	
Do I know why? What was happening at the time?	
How did I feel at these times?	
Is there anything else that I've learned?	

Recording self-criticism for one week

In order to help you to begin to step back from your self-criticism it can be helpful to notice how often it is happening. Keep a tally chart, where, for example, IIII = 4, of how many times you get caught up in self-criticism over one week.

Week starting: _____

	Morning	Afternoon	Evening	Night-time
Monday				
Tuesday				
Wednesday				
Thursday				
Friday				
Saturday				
Sunday				

When did I have the *most* self-critical thoughts?	
Do I know why? What was happening at the time?	
How did I feel at these times?	
When did I have the *fewest* self-critical thoughts?	
Do I know why? What was happening at the time?	
How did I feel at these times?	
Is there anything else that I've learned?	
What have I learned? How can I use what I've learned? What will I do?	

Answering self-critical thoughts

Identify some of the self-critical thoughts which you tend to have. Use the following questions to help identify more compassionate responses to each thought.

- What is a more compassionate and caring thought/viewpoint?
- What would I say to a friend who had this thought?
- What would a friend/family member say to me if they knew I was having this thought?
- What strengths and resources do I have which I might be overlooking?
- Am I judging myself harshly?
- Am I blaming myself for something that isn't my fault?
- Am I seeing specific difficulties as indicating my overall self-worth?
- If I have done something wrong, what can I reasonably do to make up for it?

Self-critical thoughts	Alternative compassionate thoughts

What have I learned? How can I use what I've learned? What will I do?

Evaluating my self-worth

Where would you rate your self-worth on a scale of 0% to 100%? Put a mark on the line below to represent this:

0% _____ 100%

Below are some ideas of what might make up a person's self-worth. Rate yourself from 0% to 100 on these scales by putting a mark on the lines. Add any other aspects which you use to evaluate your self-worth.

Relationships
0% _____ 100%

Work/Employment
0% _____ 100%

Health
0% _____ 100%

Hobbies/Interests
0% _____ 100%

Finances
0% _____ 100%

Religion/Spirituality
0% _____ 100%

Personality
0% _____ 100%

_____
0% _____ 100%

_____
0% _____ 100%

Now re-rate where you would put yourself on the 0% to 100% scale by taking an average of all the marks you have made. Put a mark on the line below to represent this.

0% _____ 100%

Am I putting too much emphasis on a few areas on which I rate myself lower?
Am I not putting enough emphasis on the areas on which I rate myself higher?
What have I learned? How can I use what I've learned? What will I do?

Identifying good things about me

Answer the following questions in order to identify some of the good things about you.

What good qualities do I have?

What do I like about myself?

What good things would my family say about me?

What good things would my friends and/or colleagues say about me?

What am I good at doing?

What have I achieved in my life?

Having answered all of these questions, how would I summarise what's good about me?

If I believed more that these good things about me are true, how would my life be different? What would I be thinking, feeling and doing?

Building up evidence of my good points

Whenever you do something that you or someone else might think to be positive, note it down and think about what good things it says about you. For example, saying 'hello' to a neighbour suggests that you are a friendly person.

Date	Situation – what did I do?	What does this say about me?

What have I learned? How can I use what I've learned? What will I do?

Keeping a sleep diary

Note down the following things and then use the following *Analysing my sleep diary* worksheet.

Date	Important events in the day	Time I went to bed	Time I got up in the morning	Number of hours I slept	Number of times I woke up	What I did when awake	How awake I felt the next day (0–10)	How well I performed the next day (0–10)

Analysing my sleep diary

After you have completed a sleep diary, answer the following questions:

What time do I tend to go to bed?	
What time do I tend to get out of bed?	
How many hours' sleep am I getting in a night on average?	hours on average
How many times am I waking up in the night on average?	times per night on average

What things am I tending to do when I wake up in the night?

Which of these things seem to be helpful, that is, I get back to sleep?	
Which are unhelpful, that is, I stay awake for a while?	
How awake do I tend to be the next day, out of 10?	
How well do I tend to perform the next day, out of 10?	

What tends to happen in the day which then leads to less sleep than average?

What tends to happen in the day which then leads to more sleep than average?

Are the number of hours I sleep and the number of times I wake up related to how awake I feel the next day and how well I perform?

How many hours sleep do I need to feel awake enough and to perform well enough?

What have I learned? How can I use what I've learned? What will I do?

References

Beck AT (1963) 'Thinking and depression: idiosyncratic content and cognitive distortions', *Archives of General Psychiatry*, 9, pp324–33.

Beck AT (1964) 'Thinking and depression: theory and therapy', *Archives of General Psychiatry*, 10, pp561–71.

Beck AT, Rush AJ, Shaw BF & Emery G (1979) *Cognitive Therapy of Depression*, Guildford Press, New York.

Ellis A (1957) 'Rational psychotherapy and individual psychology', *Journal of Individual Psychology*, 13, pp38–44.

Ellis A (1961) *A Guide to Rational Living*, Prentice-Hall, Englewood Cliffs, N.J.

Ellis A (2001) *Overcoming Destructive Beliefs, Feelings, and Behaviors: New Directions for Rational Emotive Behavior Therapy*, Prometheus Books, New York.

National Institute for Health and Clinical Excellence (NICE) (2004a) *Anxiety: management of anxiety (panic disorder, with or without agoraphobia, and generalised anxiety disorder) in adults in primary, secondary and community care*, online, www.nice.org.uk/guidance/CG22 (accessed 19 August 2009).

National Institute for Health and Clinical Excellence (2004b) *Depression: management of depression in primary and secondary care – NICE guidance*, online, www.nice.org.uk/guidance/CG23 (accessed 19 August 2009).

National Institute for Health and Clinical Excellence (NICE) (2005a) *Obsessive-compulsive disorder: core interventions in the treatment of obsessive-compulsive disorder and body dysmorphic disorder*, online, www.nice.org.uk/guidance/CG31 (accessed 19 August 2009).

National Institute for Health and Clinical Excellence (NICE) (2005b) *Post-traumatic stress disorder (PTSD): the management of PTSD in adults and children in primary and secondary care*, online, www.nice.org.uk/guidance/CG26 (accessed 19 August 2009).

Roth A & Fonagy P (2004) *What Works For Whom? A Critical Review of Psychotherapy Research*, 2nd edn, Guildford Press, New York.

Index

A

activity 2, 60, 71, 72, 78–85, 117
- diary, 72, 73, 79, 81
- graded, 60, 73, 83
- predicting pleasure and achievement, 73, 82, 83
- questions for identifying, 73, 81, 82
- unhelpful thoughts, 72, 73, 76–78, 85

advantages/disadvantages of belief 21, 22, 25, 26, 63–65
- coping strategy, 17, 23, 24, 28, 29, 53–55
- making changes, 21, 24–26, 65–69

anxiety 2, 3, 87–145
- analysing a fear, 88, 99, 100
- drawing out experiences of, 88, 97, 98
- evaluating the probability of fears, 88, 101
- exposure to feared situations, 89, 103
- imagining the worst, 92, 102
- relaxation diary, 89, 107
- safety behaviours – experimenting with, 89, 106
- safety behaviours – identifying, 89, 104
- safety behaviours – listing, 89, 105
- symptom checklist, 88, 108, 110

assessment headings 6, 8, 9

assumptions 25, 26, 28–31, 39, 52, 61–65, 67, 68
- advantages and disadvantages, 25, 26, 63
- building up evidence, 22, 26, 36, 39, 41, 43, 65, 90, 92, 94, 95, 125, 130, 133, 136, 149, 157
- daily record, 26, 66
- evaluating the past differently, 25, 68
- helpful memories, 26, 67
- imagining the effects, 25, 64
- identifying, 24, 53
- role play, 26, 69
- summarising changes, 26, 65

attention 2, 8, 39, 59, 137

audio-video feedback 95, 138

B

behavioural experiments 23, 49–52
- carrying out, 23, 24, 49
- recording multiple, 23, 50
- survey, 23, 51

beliefs 25, 26, 28–31, 39, 52, 61–65, 67, 68
- advantages and disadvantages, 25, 26, 63
- building up evidence, 22, 26, 36, 39, 41, 43, 65, 90, 92, 94, 95, 125, 130, 133, 136, 149, 157
- daily record, 26, 66
- evaluating the past differently, 25, 68
- helpful memories, 26, 67
- identifying, 24, 53
- imagining the effects, 25, 64
- role play, 26, 69
- summarising changes, 26, 65

blueprint, see summarising therapy

C

catastrophising 39, 41, 89, 102, 104, 105
- evaluating, 89, 105
- identifying, 89, 104
- imagining the worst, 89, 102

checklists for symptoms 32, 72, 88, 90, 92, 93, 95, 148
- anxiety, 88, 108, 110
- depression, 72, 75
- generalised anxiety disorder, 90, 112
- health anxiety, 93, 130
- low self-esteem, 148, 151
- obsessive-compulsive disorder, 92, 120
- panic, 90, 108
- post-traumatic stress disorder, 96, 139
- social anxiety, 91, 130

compulsions 2, 3, 92, 93, 120–123, 128
- diary of changes in compulsions, 93, 128
- diary of compulsions, 92, 122, 123
- diary of not neutralising, 93, 129
- diary of obsessions and compulsions, 92, 121

coping strategies 2, 8, 17, 27–29, 31, 36, 41, 49, 53–56, 74, 97, 100, 109, 143, 150
- advantages/disadvantages, 24, 55
- diary, 24, 54
- identifying, 24, 53
- testing out, 24, 56

D

depression 2, 3, 71–85
- activity diary, 72, 79
- activity diary – evaluation and questions, 73, 81
- disrupting rumination, 72, 78
- graded activity, 73, 82, 83
- predicting pleasure and achievement, 73, 83
- rumination diaries, 72, 76, 77
- symptom checklist, 72, 75
- unhelpful thoughts, 73, 76–78

diaries 22–26, 40, 50, 54, 59, 66, 72, 76, 77, 79, 81, 89, 91, 92, 93, 95, 107, 113, 114, 116, 118, 121, 129, 135, 140, 148, 149, 152, 153, 158
 activities, 72, 79, 81
 anxiety, 89, 107
 attention, 25, 59
 behavioural experiments, 50
 coping strategies, 54
 depression, 76–78
 not neutralising, 93, 129
 obsessions and compulsions, 92, 121
 relaxation, 89, 107
 rumination, 72, 76, 77
 self-criticism, 148, 152, 153
 sleep, 149, 158
 social anxiety, 95, 135
 thought distortions, 22, 40
 thoughts, 26, 66
 triggers to trauma memories, 140
 worry, 113, 114, 116, 118

distraction 60, 116, 117

E

evaluating assumptions/beliefs 22, 25, 26, 36, 39, 41, 43, 63, 65, 68, 90, 92, 94, 95, 125, 130, 133, 136, 149, 157

evaluating thoughts 22, 25, 26, 36, 39, 41, 43, 63, 65, 68, 90, 92, 94, 95, 125, 130, 133, 136, 149, 157

exposure 24, 56, 58, 89, 92, 103, 106, 126
 ladder of graded behaviours, 24, 57, 58
 recording exposure tasks, 89, 92, 93, 103, 126, 129
 recording graded tasks, 90, 106
 to thoughts, 126, 192
 without neutralising intrusions, 93, 129

F

fear, see anxiety

G

generalised anxiety disorder 2, 90, 91, 112–119
 evaluating how realistic worries are, 91, 118
 symptom checklist, 90, 112
 times for worrying, 91, 117
 tolerating uncertainty, 91, 119
 understanding worry, 91, 115
 what to do about my worries, 91, 116
 worry records, 91, 113, 114, 116, 118

goals 3, 6, 9, 11, 12, 15, 16, 41
 reviewing, 6, 12, 15
 setting, 6, 11, 16, 41

H

health anxiety 93, 94, 130–133
 alternative explanations, 94, 131, 133
 seriousness of symptoms, 94, 132
 symptom checklist, 93, 130

hypochondriasis, see health anxiety

I

images 2, 8, 10, 23, 47, 48
 preparing to change, 23, 47
 recording changes, 23, 48

intrusive thoughts 92, 93, 121, 124–127, 129
 diary of not neutralising, 93, 129
 diary of obsessions and compulsions, 92, 121
 exposure to, 92, 126
 fears/beliefs about intrusive thoughts, 92, 126
 testing out consequences of, 93, 127

L

low self-esteem 148–157
 evaluating self-worth, 148, 149, 155
 good things about someone, 149, 156, 157
 responding to self-criticism, 148, 149, 154
 self-criticism diary, 148, 152, 153
 symptom checklist, 148, 151

N

neutralising 92, 93, 127, 129
 diary of not neutralising 93, 129

O

obsessive-compulsive disorder 2, 3, 92, 93, 120–129
 diary of compulsions, 93, 128
 diary of not neutralising, 93, 129
 diary of obsessions and compulsions, 92, 121
 evaluating alternative explanations for difficulties, 92, 125
 exposure to intrusive thoughts, 92, 126
 fears/beliefs about intrusive thoughts, 92, 124
 self-therapy, 92, 93, 126, 127
 symptom checklist, 92, 120
 testing out consequences of intrusive thoughts, 93, 127

P

panic 2, 3, 90, 108–111
 diary, 90, 109
 fears of physical sensations, 90, 110
 symptom checklist, 90, 108
 testing out physical sensations, 90, 111

pie chart for responsibility 46

post-traumatic stress disorder 3, 96, 139–145
 guilt, 96, 139, 144, 145
 memories, 96, 141–143
 symptom checklist, 96, 139
 triggers, 96, 141

preparing for next therapy session 6, 13

preparing for therapy 6, 10

probability of fears 101, 118

problem solving 33, 98, 115, 116

problems and goals list 6, 11

R

relapse prevention, see setbacks

resilience 20, 28, 29, 31

response prevention, see neutralising

responsibility pie chart 46

rituals, see compulsions

role play for beliefs 26, 69

rumination 72, 76–78
    diary, 72, 76, 77
    disrupting, 72, 78

S

safety behaviours 89, 97, 104–106, 137
    experimenting with, 89, 106
    identifying, 89, 104
    listing, 89, 105

self-esteem, see low self-esteem

setbacks 7, 14, 17

sleep
    diary, 158
    analysing the sleep diary, 159

social anxiety
    diary, 95, 135
    evaluating thoughts, 85
    self-focus, 137
    symptom checklist, 93, 130

stress, see anxiety

summarising therapy 6, 7, 16, 18

surveys 23, 52

symptom checklists, see checklists for symptoms

T

thought distortions 36, 38–46, 85, 136
    diary, 22, 40
    evaluating, 22, 41, 42
    list, 21, 39

thoughts 2, 8, 11, 12, 17, 27, 30, 31, 34–45, 47–51, 62, 73, 75–77, 85, 97, 104, 106, 109, 110, 120
    diary, 26, 34, 35, 40, 66
    evaluating, 21–23, 25, 26, 36–38, 40–45

trauma, see post-traumatic stress disorder

triggers 8, 14, 32, 141

V

video feedback, see audio-video feedback

W

worry, see generalised anxiety disorder